THE CATHOLIC UNIVERSITY OF AMERICA
CANON LAW STUDIES
No. 176

PARISH SOCIETIES

BY

REV. THOMAS J. CLARKE, J.C.L.
Priest of the Diocese of Indianapolis

A DISSERTATION

Submitted to the Faculty of the School of Canon Law of the Catholic University of America in Partial Fulfillment of the Requirements for the Degree of Doctor of Canon Law

THE CATHOLIC UNIVERSITY OF AMERICA PRESS
WASHINGTON, D. C.
1943

Nihil Obstat:

HIERONYMUS D. HANNAN, S.T.D., J.C.D.,
Censor Deputatus.

Imprimatur:

✠ JOSEPH E. RITTER, D.D.;
Episcopus Indianapolitanus.

May 3, 1943.

Printed by
THE PAULIST PRESS
New York, N. Y.

 51

TO

HIS EXCELLENCY

THE MOST REVEREND JOSEPH E. RITTER, D.D.

BISHOP OF INDIANAPOLIS

TABLE OF CONTENTS

CHAPTER VI

CHAPTER VII

CHAPTER VIII

CHAPTER IX

CHAPTER X

FOREWORD

The Church was founded by Christ as an hierarchical organization. It embraces both the clergy and the laity. Both elements are necessary. And although the laity are under the direction of the clergy, it has ever been the part of the laity to assist the clergy in sustaining the life of the Church by active participation in her work. This is especially evident in the numerous societies that have existed in the Church since the earliest ages.

At the present time the number of lay societies is indeed large. Pope Pius XI has called them "precious auxiliaries of Catholic Action." Through them the faithful not only give honor to God through the increase of public worship but also manifest in a special way the charity of Christ toward one another. Since both the honor of God and the love of neighbor are essential parts of Christianity, and since these two elements form the purpose or the end for which most societies in the Church have been founded, it follows that these societies furnish an excellent means of expression for Catholic Action. Since Catholic Action has been stressed so frequently in the past few years, a study of the lay societies, or parish societies, which consist of societies of the laity working in the parish, may prove to be of some benefit.

Not much has been written upon the subject of lay societies, although ecclesiastical confraternities, sodalities, etc., have not infrequently been the subject of discussion. This is not surprising, for only ecclesiastical associations have been given specific consideration in the law of the Church. However, the prominent part that lay societies have played in the Church, the good so often and so abundantly accomplished by these societies through works of piety and charity, and the zeal of the faithful so frequently portrayed in these works, merit a breaking of the silence which has so long been kept about them.

It is true that ecclesiastical societies should be preferred to lay societies. But often such societies are not adequate. It may be wiser on the part of the Church to permit a lay society to spring up and to fulfill some need rather than to erect officially a society whose worth has not been tested. Besides, the changing conditions of our age present a variety of needs, many of which may be better fulfilled by lay societies than, perhaps, by an undesirable or even harmful multiplication of ecclesiastical associations.

The present study, then, is an attempt both to trace the historical development of lay societies and to determine their status in view of the present Church law. It is hoped that by a close definition of the exact juridic status of lay societies there will be offered a useful aid in retaining the activities of these societies within the confines of the law. It is desired, also, that present-day lay societies may continue not only to emulate the good which has been accomplished by such societies in the past, but also to reach out after still greater beneficial results which lie within the power of their accomplishment in the future.

The author wishes to express his sincere gratitude to His Excellency, the Most Reverend Joseph E. Ritter, Bishop of Indianapolis, who has made possible for him the pursuit of graduate studies at the Catholic University of America, and to the members of the Faculty of the School of Canon Law for their helpful direction and kind assistance.

CHAPTER I

PRELIMINARY NOTIONS

Article 1. Name and Definition of a Society

The word *association* is used by the Code of Canon Law as a designation for different kinds of societies, and hence as a generic word.[1] The Code also uses the words *sodality* and *confraternity* in a generic sense, despite the fact that it likewise has given to each of these a specific definition.[2] In the acts of the Councils a great number of words have been used to designate societies or confraternities,[3] and even in the decisions of the Roman Congregations no uniformity has existed either before[4] or after[5] the Code.

It is a universally acknowledged truism that a name is given to a person or to an object with the avowed logical purpose of identifying or of characterizing the person or the object. Groups of people bound together for some specific purpose evidently were characterized with specific names in view of the manner in which they were united, from the consideration of the end for which they were united, or on account of some other relevant reason. However, early societies in the Church never received any definite or permanent standing. As a result numerous and varied societies were estab-

[1] Canons 700; 701; 707, § 1; 685; 686, etc.

[2] Canon 707. Cf. canons 383, § 1; 913, 3°; 1356, § 1; 1653, § 3.

[3] Some of the more common words used are *Fratantiae, Confratantiae, Confraternitates, Congregationes, Collegia, Sodalitates, Societates, Scholae,* etc. There are many others, but their use is somewhat less common. Cf. Ebner, *Die klösterlichen Gebetsverbrüderungen* (Regensburg, 1890), pp. 3-6.

[4] S. C. Ep. et Reg., *Romana,* 18 ian. 1907: "Porro vox confraternitatis in iure determinatum sensum non habet, quum etiam pro pia unione, congregatione, et pio opere usurpetur. . . ."—*Codicis Iuris Canonici Fontes cura Emi. Petri Card. Gasparri editi* (9 vols., Romae, 1923-1939), n. 2054. This collection will henceforth be cited simply as *Fontes.*

[5] S. C. C., *Corrienten.,* 13 nov. 1920: ". . . in qua divisione (confraternitas) sumitur pro qualibet societate seu associatione in finem inita. . . ."—*AAS,* XIII (1921), 139.

lished. Their form or purpose often changed,[6] different societies took on different works, societies instituted for a specific purpose broadened their work and became assimilated with others. As a consequence names given to specific societies became applicable to others, and soon came to be used indiscriminately for all.[7]

The broadest term used in Title XVIII of Book II of the Code is the word *association.* It can be defined as a voluntary union, more or less permanently established, of a number of persons striving under their properly constituted leaders for the attainment of a common objective.[8] The term *society* is used in the Code as generally and as broadly as, and probably more commonly than, the word *association.* The term *confraternity* is somewhat less broad in its meaning since the promulgation of the Code, inasmuch as present law does not recognize some of the divisions of confraternities as made before the Code.[9] However, the terminology cannot be ignored, since some of the confraternities now existing received their designation under the old law.[10]

Furthermore, even though the term is becoming more specific through the present usage, there remains its former generic application which still persists and which renders any attempt to restrict its meaning useless in the study of the history of societies. There-

[6] Paulus III, Const. *"Altitudo Divinae Providentiae,"* 7 febr. 1541: "Concedimus facultatem plenam ac liberam mutare, alterare, limitare, corrigere, declarare, modificare, et in melius reformare. . . ."—*Bullarium Diplomatum et Privilegiorum Sanctorum Romanorum Pontificum Taurinensis Editio* (24 vols. et Appendix, Neapoli, 1857-1872), VI, 307-312. Hereafter this collection will be cited as *Bull. Rom.*

[7] S. C. Indulg., *Urbis et Orbis,* 26 nov. 1880, ad III: ". . . aequum est distinguere inter Sodalitia, quae strictiori sensu collegia dici possunt, ut esse solent pleraeque proprii nominis Confraternitates ad modum organici corporis constitutae, et Sodalitia, quae laxiori modo sociali vinculo colligantur, ut esse solent plures etiam Confraternitates. . . ."—*Decreta Authentica Sacrae Congregationis Indulgentiis Sacrisque Reliquiis* (Romae: Ratisbonae, 1883), n. 453. This collection will be cited *Decr. Auth.* Cf. also *Fontes,* n. 5090.

[8] ". . . eine auf Dauer berechnete, freiwillege Verbingung einer Mehrzahl von Personen, um unter Leitung einen von den Mitgliedern bestimmten gemeinschaftlichen Zweck zu verwirklichen und zu fördern."—Beil, *Das kirchliche Vereinsrecht* (Paderborn: Schöningh, 1932), pp. 32-33.

[9] Cf. *supra,* footnote 7.

[10] This is true especially in Italy, Portugal, and in some parts of France.

fore, in the history the words *confraternity* and *society* will be used in a generic sense for any association or union of a number of the faithful formed freely under properly instituted leadership for at least a partially religious purpose. However, in the commentary no other term will be used for lay societies except the terms *society* and *associations,* which latter term refers to both lay and ecclesiastical societies. The terms *confraternity, sodality,* and *pious unions* will refer only to ecclesiastical associations.

Article 2. Division

An association or society is either *ecclesiastical* or *lay* in its character. An *ecclesiastical* society is a free union of the faithful established or approved [11] by ecclesiastical authority for the exercise of some work of piety or of charity not prescribed for all the faithful.[12] The Code acknowledges for societies of this nature the characteristic of juridic personality when through a decree of the ordinary, who has the right to erect them, they have been constituted as moral persons in the Church.[13] Before the advent of the Code this same term, *ecclesiastical society,* was indeed used, but not in such a strict sense. Those confraternities which were not erected by at least a bishop were known as *pious* or *lay societies.*[14]

Ecclesiastical societies are divided in the Code into (a) *third orders secular,* which consist of persons who, though living in the world, strive for Christian perfection under the moderation of some order and according to its spirit,[15] and (b) *pious unions,* which are associations of the faithful erected for the exercise of some work of piety or of charity.[16] Pious unions, constituted with an internal

[11] Canon 686, § 1.

[12] Schaefer, *De Religiosis* (3. ed., Romae: Typis Polyglottis Vaticanis, 1940), n. 612.

[13] Canon 687.

[14] Schmalzgrueber, *Ius Ecclesiasticum Universum* (5 vols. in 12, Romae, 1843-1845), lib. III, tit. 36, n. 2; Reiffenstuel, *Ius Canonicum Universum* (5 vols. in 7, Parisiis, 1864-1882), lib. III, tit. 36, n. 7.

[15] Canon 702, § 1.

[16] Canon 707, § 1.

hierarchical organization,[17] are called *sodalities*.[18] And a sodality which has as its specific end the increase and enhancement of public worship is called a *confraternity*.[19] Hence, in a strict sense, a confraternity is an association of the faithful erected as an hierarchical organization for the exercise of the specific work of piety, the increase of public worship.

The Code, then, distinguishes between two generic associations, the *third orders secular* and *pious unions*. The former have no divisions but the latter admit of two species, *sodalities* and *confraternities*. Both the terms, *sodality* and *confraternity*, are sometimes used in a generic sense [20] but are, in a strict sense, only species of pious unions.

By reason of their origin, societies are divided into *papal, diocesan* or *religious* societies,[21] inasmuch as they were instituted by the Pope, a Bishop, or a religious superior. Among the latter are included the third orders.[22]

A *lay* society is any association or pious union to which no official ecclesiastical recognition has been given. It is one which is governed and directed primarily by the laity.[23] Such societies may be classified as:

(a) *Recommended* societies, which, although not established or formally approved by ecclesiastical authority, have received its recommendation or praise;

[17] The Code uses the words *ad modum organici corporis*. This indicates an authoritative "head," officers, constitution, by-laws, etc.

[18] Canon 707, § 1.

[19] Canon 707, § 2.

[20] Canon 697, § 1; cf. *supra*, footnote 5.

[21] The word "religious" here is not to be understood in the sense of canon 487, nor is the term "religious society" to be understood in the sense of canon 488. These terms do not refer to those who strive after a more perfect life through the observance, by vow, of the evangelical counsels.

[22] Before the Code religious of simple vows, in canonical language, were called *sodales*, and the institutes were termed *sodalitates piae*. Cf. S. C. Ep. et Reg., *Congregationis Presbyterorum Saecularium*, 16 sept. 1864—*Fontes*, n. 1993.

[23] S. C. C., *Corrienten*, 13 nov. 1920: ". . . confraternitates laicales et ecclesiasticae non distinguuntur a fine, sed ex eo quod primae laicales dirigantur et gubernentur a personis laicis; aliae ecclesiasticae ab auctoritate ecclesiastica."—*AAS*, XIII (1921), 139; Schaefer, *De Religiosis*, n. 612.

(b) *Licit* societies, which, neither approved nor recommended, nevertheless are not contrary to the laws of God or of the Church, and have as their end works of piety and charity, even though not exclusively so;

(c) *Illicit* societies, among which are included the condemned, secret, and suspected societies.

Finally societies, both ecclesiastical and lay, can be divided by reason of their *constitution* and by reason of the *territory* in which they are located. By reason of their *constitution* they are either *incorporated,*[24] that is, a plurality of persons, possessing corporate rights, and acknowledged by law,[25] or *non-incorporated,* that is, not possessing any legal recognition. A corporation in Canon Law is known as a moral person.[26] Whether or not a society is erected as a moral person, it can still be erected *ad modum organici corporis,* that is, having a hierarchical organization with the subordination of its members to lawfully constituted superiors within the society.[27] Otherwise it is a simple union whose members are loosely bound by having assumed in common certain obligations, and by enjoying in virtue of their membership certain privileges and spiritual benefits.[28]

An ecclesiastical moral person can be *collegiate* or *non-collegiate* in character. A collegiate moral person is one whose members are imbued with equal rights and obligations arising from the union of the members themselves. In a non-collegiate moral person the sum of the rights and obligations is invested in some moral entity.[29] An example of this latter is a parish, hospital, orphanage, an endowment

[24] The words *incorporated* and *corporation* are used to refer to an ecclesiastical moral person and are not to be confused with the manner in which the persons are united as in sodalities erected *ad modum organici corporis*. These latter are sometimes called *corporate bodies*.

[25] Augustine, *A Commentary on the New Code of Canon Law* (8 vols., St. Louis-London: B. Herder Book Co.), Vol. II (6. ed., 1936), 1-2.

[26] Canon 99.

[27] "Sodalitium ist eine Körperschaft, ein organisierter Verein, d.h., eine Kollektiveinheit mit statutarisch geregelter Über-und Unterordnung."—Beil, *Das kirchliche Vereinsrecht,* p. 48.

[28] ". . . die Gesellschaft ist eine durch gegenseitige Obligation verbundene Vielheit."—Beil, *loc. cit.* Cf. can. 686, § 3.

[29] Jone, *Gesetzbuch der kanonischen Rechtes* (3 vols., Paderborn: Schöningh, 1939-1940), I, under canon 99.

and such like, which, although governed or administered by a superintendent, president, or rector,[30] nevertheless has its juridic entity from the law or the ecclesiastical authority which grants and recognizes it and not from the physical persons connected with or attached to it.[31] Both a collegiate and a non-collegiate moral person become extinct through suppression by legitimate authority or, by the law itself, when it has lapsed from tangible existence for a period of a hundred years.[32] Ecclesiastical societies, therefore, can be either collegiate or non-collegiate moral persons if they exist for a religious or charitable purpose and if ecclesiastical authority, by a formal decree, has erected them as such. However lay societies can be neither collegiate nor non-collegiate moral persons. For if they were erected as such by a formal decree they would *ipso iure* become ecclesiastical in character [33] and thereby lose their lay character.

By reason of the *territory* in which they are located, societies are either *universal,* that is, established for the whole catholic world, or *regional,* that is, instituted for a certain city or parish.[34] In a society established for the whole world any Catholic, all things being equal, would have the right to become a member, while only those who live in the locality where it is established could join a regional or local society. Furthermore, a parish society need not be confined to a single parish. The same society may exist in another parish, or in all the parishes of a diocese, and still not be diocesan or regional, because it was not instituted as such.

Other divisions can be found, such as those which are derived from the twofold purpose of societies to provide either for some special need, *e. g.,* the Holy Name Society, or some special work, *e. g.,* the St. Vincent de Paul Society. But the end for which a society is founded is immaterial in the present connection as long as it is of a religious or pious nature. Furthermore, some societies are called *general,* such as the Christian Mother's Society, which has

[30] Canons 1409-1494.

[31] Jone, *loc. cit.*

[32] Canon 102, § 2.

[33] Canon 687. Since lay societies can be incorporated in civil law this point is treated in the chapter on *The Establishment of Parish Societies.* Cf. *infra,* pp. 40-41.

[34] S. C. Indulg., 26 ian. 1871—*Decr. Auth.,* n. 428; *Fontes,* n. 5079.

spread to other countries, and some are designated as *special* societies, such as the Church Extension Society, which is peculiar to the United States of America. This division also is immaterial inasmuch as the territory through which a society is spread or to which it is restricted does not change the nature of that society or give it any ecclesiastical approval.

Article 3. Scope of Present Study—Lay Societies

The present study treats of *recommended* [85] and *licit lay societies*. Since they have not received ecclesiastical approval they are sometimes called *private* lay societies. In this sense the word *private* does not indicate any restriction of membership or any other similar kind of exclusiveness. Rather it points to an unofficial status in opposition to the status of public or official recognition. But since the word *lay* distinguishes them sufficiently from the approved ecclesiastical societies, the word *private* seems to be superfluous.

In the present connection also the term *lay* is used differently than in canon 488, 4°, and canon 948 of the Code,[86] inasmuch as it does not refer to the character or state of life of the members who belong to the society, but rather to the authority by which the society exists.[87] Thus any society which is not established by the public ecclesiastical authority in the Church is designated in the law as a lay society whether it is formed by the clergy or by the laity.

Throughout the historical conspectus they shall simply be called *confraternities* or *societies*, not only because they were more frequently designated by these terms in the past, but also because no more specific or definite name was given to them in designation of their particular lay character. The fact that they were instituted with or without the permission of ecclesiastical authority had no

[85] What constitutes a *recommended* society is treated in connection with the establishment of parish societies. Cf. *infra*, pp. 35-36.

[86] In canon 488 the Code applies the word *lay* to a religious house or community the majority of whose members are not priests. Such a community is called a *lay religious society*. In canon 948 the word *lay* refers to all who are not clerics, thus distinguishing the clergy from the laity.

[87] Cf. Beringer-Steinen, *Die Ablässe, Ihr Wesen und Gebrauch* (2 vols., Paderborn: Schöningh, 1921-1922), I, 9, footnote 9; Beil, *Das kirchliche Vereinsrecht*, p. 29.

effect or influence upon names given to them. The term *lay* is simply a more or less recent designation given to those societies which are established without ecclesiastical authority to distinguish them from those which are established with that authority. However, since all the early societies sprang up without this authority, the word *lay* rightly seems to apply to all of them.

In later times and especially with the advent of the Code, societies came to be regarded as being either ecclesiastical or lay in character. Ecclesiastical societies are excluded from the scope of this study which is concerned only with lay societies.

CHAPTER II

ORIGIN AND DEVELOPMENT OF SOCIETIES

THE establishment of the Church brought into being a supernatural organization with a supernatural law above the law of the State. It effected a separation between the Church law and State law. Hence it implied the formation of a new perfect society.[1] This society effected essential changes in the quality of individuals. Christ's gospel abolished the Roman legal distinctions between the free and the slave, the citizen and the foreigner, and established one equal citizenship in Christ's social order. The propagation of the faith began with the conversion of 3,000 by St. Peter "when the days of Pentecost were accomplished." [2] Although the Church spread rapidly throughout Judea, Galilee, Samaria, and to all the parts of the civilized world, it remained dependent upon the Church of Jerusalem.[3] Thus its unity as an independent society was maintained. While the persecutions did indeed present an obstacle to the free functioning of this society, yet that obstacle was not insurmountable. The early Christians were wont to gather in private homes, in the catacombs, and in places sanctified by the prayers and the blood of the martyrs to offer their prayers and to celebrate the Eucharist. While these gatherings cannot be considered as connoting the beginning of societies within the Church, they nevertheless were the seeds from which such societies sprang, as they proved to be the outward expressions of the faith sanctioned indeed by Christ when He said: "Where two or three are gathered together for My sake, there am I in the midst of them." [4]

[1] Ottaviani, *Institutiones Iuris Publici Ecclesiastici* (2. ed., E Civitate Vaticana: Typis Polyglottis Vaticanis, 1935-1936), I, 185-209.

[2] Acts of the Apostles, II, 1.

[3] Cf. the historical narrative of the Council of Jerusalem in the *Acts of the Apostles,* Chapter XV.

[4] Matt. XVIII, 20.

Article 1. Early Roman Societies

The earliest evidence of societies within the Roman Empire is furnished by the *collegia tenuiorum,* which were generally a group of poor people legally bound by Roman law,[5] whose purpose was to assist one another in time of need and especially to provide for a proper funeral rite and burial. These *collegia* possibly served the Church in an indirect way to accomplish with Roman legal aid and recognition what the Church could otherwise not have accomplished with the protection of the Roman law as long as its juridical entity was unacknowledged by the Roman State. But nothing further can be ascertained. These societies were thought by some authors to have been the means with which the Church acquired a juridical standing in the Roman Empire. However, no documents which would have been necessary for the propagation of all the churches in this legal form are found. Nor is there any evidence of any ecclesiastical approbation given to them. The most that can be concluded with certainty is that these *collegia* existed among the faithful in some parts of the Church as private societies for the purpose of performing works of mutual helpfulness with the legal approval and protection of the law of the Roman state.[6]

In the Orient there is found evidence of societies or confraternities, the members of which are known as the *parabalanin.* They occupied a rank among the members of the clergy,[7] and their purpose was especially to care for the sick.[8] Their number was determined by law,[9] probably to conform to the needs which these societies ful-

[5] D (3. 4) 1; D (47. 22) 1.

[6] ". . . sed permittitur tenuioribus stipem menstruam conferre dum tamen semel in mense coeant, . . . quod non tantum in urbe sed et in Italia et in provinciis locum habere divus quoque Severus rescripsit."—D (47. 22) 1. The law referred to was enacted by Septimius Severus (193-211).

[7] "Placet nostrae clementiae, ut nihil commune clerici cum publicis actibus, vel ad curiam pertinentibus, cuius corpori non sunt annexi, habeant. Praetera his, qui parabalanin vocantur neque ad quodlibet publicum spectaculum neque ad curiae locum neque ad iudicium accedendi licentiam permittimus. . . ."—C (1. 3) 17.

[8] "Parabalanin, qui ad curanda debilium aegra corpora deputantur. . . ."—C (1. 3) 18; C. Th. (16. 2) 43. The date of this law is Feb. 3, 418.

[9] "Praeterea eis, qui parabalani vocantur non plus quingentos esse praecipi-

filled. Another group known as the *lecticarii*[10] included also laymen. Similar to these was the *college of Deans* which existed at Constantinople to serve definite purposes in connection with the burial of the dead.[11] However, there is no evidence to prove that any of these societies possessed ecclesiastical sanction. Nor are there any grounds upon which to base the assumption that they had any relationship with later societies. Evidence seems rather to point to the medieval societies as springing from the confraternities of prayer or purgatorial societies and the gilds.

Article 2. The Confraternities of Prayer or Purgatorial Societies

The confraternities of prayer, or purgatorial societies as they are sometimes called,[12] were founded chiefly, but not solely, to assist the deceased members with Masses and prayers. Indeed, it can be said that the early Church was one large purgatorial society, evidence of which is supplied by the prayers for the dead in the oldest liturgies, the breviary prayers, and by the earliest Christian inscriptions.[13] The Catholic doctrine concerning purgatory, the communion of the saints, and the satisfactory value of good works, formed the basis of these societies in the Church, although they sprang from pure

mus. . . ."—C. Th. (16. 2) 42; the date of this law is Sept. 29, 416. "Parabalanin, qui ad curanda debilium aegra corpora deputantur, sescentos constitui praecipimus. . . ."—C (1. 3) 18.

[10] "Atque sancimus mille centum officinas omnibus modis illibatas et omni praestatione immunes sanctissimae maiori ecclesiae servari decanorum seu lecticariorum et exequiarum defunctorum nomine destinatas. . . ."—N (43. 1).

[11] "Non plures quam nongenti quinquaginta decani sacrosanctae huius amplissimae urbis deputantur ecclesiae . . . : nullique alii corporatorum praeter praedictum numerum per patrocinia immunitate concessa negataque omni novationis facultate similia vindicandi his, quae in honorem vel necessaria obsequia sacrosanctae ecclesiae indulta sunt." (Sept. 12, 409)—C (1. 2) 4. Cf. also C. Th. (6. 33).

[12] *Totenbünde* was the name given by Ebner to those societies which were formed in Synods. Cf. Ebner, *Die klösterlichen Gebets-verbruderungen* (Regensburg, 1890), pp. 3-4.

[13] There is evidence of such an inscription in the Church of St. Cosmas and Damian in Rome. Cf. Baronius, *Annales Ecclesiasticae* (38 vols., Lucae, 1738-1759), XVI (1744), 272.

Christian charity which reaches beyond the grave. These societies were known to have existed in the earliest ages of the Church and were closely related to the Church itself. Nevertheless knowledge of their origin as to any one specific form is very confused.

It is obvious, therefore, that these societies did not spring into existence as societies in the very beginning but were a development of works of piety and charity and especially charity towards the dead. The first foundations of these societies are found among the members of monasteries who gathered together to offer prayers for the dead. In the early period of their existence the secular clergy were admitted to these gatherings.[14] At a later time kings, princes, noblemen, and finally all the laity were allowed to adscribe themselves to these gatherings.[15] Many of these early societies or gatherings were formed at Synods, as may be gathered from a letter of St. Boniface, written in 745 to Archbishop Egbert of York, asking that he and his co-workers be received into the *confraternity* that had been established there.[16] It is only for a later period, however, that any decrees concerning such gatherings or societies are to be found. In 762 at the Synod of Attigny the bishops and priests present obliged themselves to have one hundred Masses and psalms sung upon receiving word of the death of any of the members.[17] Similar

[14] Examples of these confraternities are found mentioned in the following Councils: Attigny (762)—*MGH, Legum Sectio III, Concilia,* Tom. II, pars 1 (recensivit Albertus Werminghoff, Hannoverae et Lipsiae, 1904), 72; Frankfort (794)—*MGH, ibid.,* p. 110; Salzburg (799)—*MGH, ibid.,* p. 205; Freising (805)—*MGH, ibid.,* p. 233.

[15] ". . . Insuper etiam unusquisque in unaquaque parochia degens die palmarum denarium unum aut potum unius denarii in elemosynam sui parentumque suorum vivorum ac mortuorum presbytero suo praesentare, illeque in cena Dominii proprio episcopo offerre studeat, quatenus inde destructe ecclesie innoventur, et lumen illorum in eis in perpetuum non extinguetur."—*MGH, Leges, III, Leges Nationum Germanicarum* (ed. G. H. Pertz, Hannoverae, 1863), 483.

[16] ". . . Nunc autem initimis praecordiorum praecibus almitatis tuae clementiam obsecro, ut vestrae fraternitatis synodo una cum servis Dei mecum laborantibus adunatus esse merear, et sis mihi consiliarius et adjutor in inquirendis et investigandis regulis ecclesiasticis judiciorum Dei."—*MGH, Epistolae Selectae,* I, *St. Bonifatii et Lulli Epistolae* (ed. Michael Tangl, Berolini, 1916), 157.

[17] ". . . quando quislibet de hoc saeculo migraverit, centum psalteria et presbiteri eius speciales misas centum cantent. Ipse autem episcopus per se 30 misas impleat; nisi infirmitate aut aliquo impedimento prohibeatur. Tunc roget

decrees were often repeated by later synods and councils. The Provincial Council of Freising in 805 had the same legislation,[18] while the Synod of Salzburg in 799 determined the method by which the members were to be notified of the death of one of their members.[19]

From this time onward other works of charity were prescribed for the members. The Provincial Council of Freising (805) prescribed the giving of alms to the poor,[20] the National Council of Tours in 859 ordered certain prayers to be said and Masses to be celebrated for the living members of the society,[21] and a confraternity established at Fulda in 863 encouraged the visiting of the sick.[22] Because of this new legislation these societies became more similar to and in some instances identified with the gilds.

Article 3. The Gilds

Gilds, though mostly private in character, did contribute much to the development of the confraternities in the Middle Ages. The name *gild* is derived by authors from the Anglo-Saxon *gyldon,* meaning *to pay,* or indicative of a *rateable payment,* because one of the distinguishing characteristics of the gilds was the payment of dues by the members.[23] Gilds owe their origin to the endeavor of the

alterum episcopum pro se cantare: abbatas vero qui non sunt episcopi . . . 30 misas expleant, et presbiteri eorum centum misas et monachi centum psalteria psallere meminerunt."—*MGH, Legum Sectio III, Leges Nationum Germanicarum,* Tom. II, pars 1, p. 72.

[18] *MGH, ibid.,* p. 479.

[19] Cap. 16: "Convenit igitur sancta synodo, ut quando quis Deo iubente de hoc saeculo migraverit . . . de ipso loco . . . dirigantur literae ad singulas domos episcopates, et ipse episcopus in diocesi sua habeat commendatum, qui ipsas litteras suscipiat, et ceteris . . . pro ipsa anima orandum litteris suis notum faciant nomen et tempus."—*MGH, Leges, I, Capitularia Regum Francorum* (ed. Pertz, 1835), 81.

[20] *MGH, Leges, III, Leges Nationum Germanicarum,* 479.

[21] Cap. 13: "Statuerent . . . ut pro se invicem omnes, dum adviverent, preces huiusmodi frequentarent; scilicet ut singuli pro cunctis per singulas hebdomadas, feria quarta, missum celebarent."—*MGH, Leges, I, Capitularia,* 465.

[22] "Si aliquis eorum languore correptus infirmetur, ceteri . . . visitent eum et solacia praebeant."—*MGH, Scriptores,* XIII (ed. G. Waitz, Hannoverae, 1881), 215.

[23] Smith, *English Gilds* (London, 1870), p. XIX.

toiling masses to free themselves from oppression. As such their origin can be traced back to early Spartan, Athenian, and Greek history.[24]

How and when the word became applied to the brotherhoods or societies is nowhere found stated in so many words, but the reason for the use of the word in designation of these societies was the practice of paying a regular rate of dues to take care of expenses.[25] It is only with Roman history, however, that the gilds reflected a religious character. And even relative to that period in history it is difficult to determine whether the gilds were not also social as well as religious.[26] Both aspects seem to be in evidence. Although the gilds may have had their origin purely for social reasons, it was not long after the foundation of Christianity that some of them assumed a purely religious character. It is safe then to say that the gilds were established primarily for secular purposes, but by medieval times never forgot in their constitutions and practical life the special works of charity for their deceased members.[27]

The early gilds were known by different names.[28] This fact makes it all the more difficult to distinguish between them and the specifically designated societies. In relation to religious societies the word is first found in the Lombardian capitulary of 799, which contains a prohibition against administering the sacraments to those who enter gilds wherein the members are bound to one another by an oath.[29] Later, in 852, Hincmar, Archbishop of Rheims, enacted the first ecclesiastical legislation on gilds,[30] which was entitled, "De

[24] *Trade Gilds of Europe,* United States Consular Reports (Washington, D. C.: Government Printing Office, 1885), pp. 3-4.

[25] Smith, *loc. cit.*

[26] Lambert, *Two Thousand Years of Gild Life* (London, 1891), p. 24.

[27] Michael, *Geschichte des deutchen Volkes* (6 vols., Freiburg in Breisgau, 1897-1915), I, 151-152. An explanation of religious gilds among the clergy is given by Lambert, who says that in the year 738 clerics and monks began to engage in various trades.—*Op. cit.*, p. 6.

[28] Beringer-Steinen, *Die Ablässe,* II, 3; Michael, *Geschichte,* I, 144.

[29] Cap. 16; "De sacramentis per gildonia invicem coniurantibus, ut nemo facere praesumat. . . . Nemo eas ad excusationem in ecclesia sua introire permittat. . . ."—*MGH, Leges, I, Capitularia,* 37.

[30] Some authors refer to this as the first legislation on confraternities. Cf. Bassi, *De Piis Sodalitiis* (Romae, 1739), p. 141.

confratriis, eorumque conventibus, quomodo celebrari debeant."[31]

Hincmar distinguished between two kinds of confraternities; one among the clergy, the other among the laity, the latter alone being known as a gild. In this treatise he gives instructions to his clergy concerning the gilds and the solemnities to be held at their meetings. First he insisted in general words that only that should be done which was required by dignity, utility, and reason, and immediately explained this by saying that members should unite for religious motives, such as that of assisting at funerals, of giving alms, and of executing other works of piety.[32] He forbade and condemned those gilds whose meetings were characterized by excessive feasting and drinking under penalty of degradation for clerics and of expulsion for the lay members. Finally he laid down some special rules for the settlement of any difficulty that might have arisen among them.[33] From this it can be seen that Hincmar endeavored to direct these gilds along religious lines, but he was not successful, as can be seen from the large number of councils that eventually prohibited membership in the gilds.[34]

In England the societies of the later Middle Ages were always

[31] Migne, *Patrologiae Cursus Completus, Series Latina* (221 vols., Paris, 1847-1870), CXXV, 777-778. Hereafter this collection will be cited as *MPL.*

[32] "Ut de collectis, quas geldonias vel confratrias vulgo vocant, sicut iam verbis monuimus, et nunc scriptis expresse praecipimus, tantum fiat, quantum ad auctoritatem et utilitatem atque rationem pertinet; ultra autem nemo neque sacerdos, neque fidelis quisquam, in parochia nostra progredi audeat. Id est in omni obsequio religionis conjungantur: videlicet in oblatione, in luminaribus, in oblationibus mutuis, in exsequiis defunctorum, in eleemosynis, et caeteris pietatis officiis. . . ."—*MPL, loc. cit.*

[33] "Pastos autem et commessationes quas divina auctoritas vetat, ubi et gravedines et indebitae exactiones, et turpes ac ananes laetitiae et rixae . . . accidere solent adeo penitus interdicimus ut qui de caetero hoc agere praesumpserit, si presbyter fuerit, vel quilibet clericus, gradu privetur, si laicus, vel femina usque ad satisfactionem separetur. . . . Si forte aliquis contra parem suum discordiam habuerit, quem reconciliari necesse sit, et sine conventu presbyteri et caeterorum esse non possit, post peracta illa quae Dei sunt, et Christianae religioni conveniunt, et post debitas admonitiones . . . et panem tantum frangentes, singuli singulos biberes accipiant, nihil amplius continguere praesumant, et sic unusquisque ad sua cum benedictione domini redeat."—*Loc. cit.*

[34] Cf. *infra*, pp. 17-18, footnotes 2 and 4.

known as gilds. Lambert lists the essential features of the English gilds:

(a) Fellowship of members confirmed by oath or promise;

(b) Regular contributions;

(c) Periodical feasting and drinking;

(d) Rules for preserving courtesy and order;

(e) Special care for the funeral rights of members and a commemoration by Masses for his soul;

(f) Other methods for caring for the needs of the poor.[35]

The same writer points to no less than six religious gilds that existed in Kingston-upon-Hull. These were the Gild of the Holy Trinity, the Gild of St. John the Baptist, the Gild of Corpus Christi, the Gild of the Blessed Virgin Mary, the Gild of St. Barbara, and the Gild of St. Clare.[36] But these gilds, which had been founded by private persons, and of which at least some had received a kind of ecclesiastical approval, probably without exception came eventually under the exclusive control of private hands. They all failed to survive the Protestant Revolt.

[35] *Op. cit.*, p. 50.

[36] *Op. cit.*, p. 111.

CHAPTER III

ECCLESIASTICAL LEGISLATION

Article 1. Prohibitive Legislation

Medieval societies, to a certain extent, were a combination of the confraternities of prayer and of the gilds.[1] The former were established primarily for religious purpose, the latter for temporal ends. The former at times lost much of their religious character, while the gilds during the early Middle Ages became entirely religious, although not unlike the confraternities of prayer they too slipped back into secular practices. The Church, being a perfect and an independent society founded by Christ to attain a supernatural end, has jurisdiction in all spiritual matters. Because these societies took upon themselves not only the works of piety and of charity, but also other works of a religious nature, they naturally fell under the legislative power of the Church. At first this legislation was almost entirely of a prohibitive nature. It represented an effort on the part of the Church to correct the abuses that had crept into these societies.

Frequently there were condemned those societies whose members were bound to one another by an oath of furnishing mutual assistance against all adversaries.[2]

Members of the laity who presumed to establish societies on their

[1] "Zwischen diesen Gebetsverbrüderungen, die mehr einen geistlichen oder selbst klösterlichen Charakter hatten, und jenen Gilder, die umgekehrt wenigstens auch weltliche Ziele verfolgten, entwickelten sich nun allmählich, ohne dass man genau die trennende, unterscheidende Linie ausfindig machen könnte, die eigentlichen kirchlichen Bruderschaften. . . ."—Beringer-Steiner, *Die Ablässe,* II, 3.

[2] Cf. Lombardian Capitulary—*MGH, Leges, I, Capitularia,* 37. For similar laws cf. *ibid.,* pp. 74; 135; 230; 232; 352; 553. Cf. also Council of Avignon (1326), can. 37—Mansi, *Sacrorum Conciliorum Nova et Amplissima Collectio,* 53 vols. in 59 (Paris, Leipzig, Arnhem, 1901-1927), XXV, 764. Hereafter this collection of the Councils will simply be cited as Mansi.

own initiative and without the consent of the ordinary were often condemned[3] and such societies themselves were condemned unless they were of an entirely religious character.[4] The use of intoxicating liquors at meetings was forbidden,[5] and generally anyone of doubtful character, especially a public sinner, was not to be accepted as a member. If one who was a member did not upon due previous warning relent, he was by the bishop's authority to be expelled.[6] No member was to be admitted unless a priest was present who imposed upon him the symbol of the confraternity,[7] nor could any election be held unless a priest appointed by the bishop was present.[8] The V Provincial Council of Milan (1579) also warned against the discussion of dogmatic questions by lay persons,[9] the collecting of alms without the permission of the ordinary, and the carrying of arms or of weapons into the meetings except when the dignity of the person or of his office warranted it.[10]

In relation to these prohibitions the *Decretum* of Gratian (c.

[3] Gregory IX, const., *"Ad Nostram,"* 26 oct. 1232—*Bull. Rom.*, III, 474; Potthast, *Regesta Pontificum Romanorum* (2 vols., Berolini, 1874-1875), n. 9026. Cf. also Provincial Council of Sens, France (1528)—Mansi, XXXII, 1196.

[4] Council of Avignon (1326), can. 37: "Per hoc autem, confratrias olim in honore Dei, et beatae Mariae, et aliorum sanctorum pro subsidiis pauperum introductas, in quibus coniurationes et iuramenta non interveniunt huiusmodi, non intendimus reprobare. . . ."—Mansi, XXV, 764. Cf. also: Council of Rouen (1189), cap. XXV—Mansi, XXII, 585; Council of Toulouse (1229), cap. XXXVIII—Mansi, XXIII, 203; Council of Arles (1234), cap. IX—Mansi, XXIII, 339; Council of Cognac (1238), cap. X—Mansi, XXIII, 494; Council of Tarragona (1239), cap. X—Mansi, XXIII, 515; Council of Bordeaux (1255), cap. XXIX, XXX—Mansi, 865.

[5] National Synod of Hungary (1114), can. 47—Mansi, XXI, 108-109.

[6] V Provincial Council of Milan (1579), Constitutionum Pars Tertia, n. XVIII: "Ne facinorosi homines, neve turpis vitae, aut infamiae labe notati, in disciplinatorum, alteriusve generis confratriis adscribantur. Si qui vero iam adscripti sunt, si moniti, honestae vitae rationibus se non conformarint, a confratrum numero, episcopali auctoritate, et cura amoveantur."—Mansi, XXXIV A, 483.

[7] V Provincial Council of Milan—*loc. cit.*

[8] *Loc. cit.*

[9] *Loc. cit.* This was but a restatement of a general law.

[10] Constitutionum Pars III, n. XVIII—Mansi, XXXIV A, 483.

1140) mentions the punishment to be inflicted upon clerics who were members of forbidden societies. It will be recalled that Hincmar legislated against those gilds in which the meetings were characterized by excessive feasting and drinking by threatening degradation for the clerics and expulsion for lay persons.[11] The pertinent legislation which was contained in the *Decretum* of Gratian forbade membership in those societies in which the members were bound to one another by oath, a law which had long been in force. The punishment for clerics was the same as that which Hincmar had threatened, namely, degradation for clerics who became members of such groups.[12]

Article 2. Affirmative Legislation

A. *Synods and Councils*

It is true that many of these prohibitions were limited to a place or to a territory which was under the jurisdiction of some particular Synod or Council. However, such laws serve to show the attitude of the Church towards societies in general. The Church never discouraged the establishment or the work of societies which prosecuted a purely religious aim or purpose but merely attempted to eradicate the abuses that continued to creep into them. As time went on societies in various forms became more numerous. More salutary legislation was enacted. Not completely successful in abolishing the condemned societies and in preventing corruptions in the licit societies by prohibitive legislation or laws the Church resorted with growing frequency to affirmative legislation as an agency for the proper regulation of societies among the members of the Church.

Rules were made concerning the establishment of societies. These rules required the consent of the ordinary and, at times, the permission of the temporal ruler.[13] The bishop had the right to examine

[11] *MPL,* CXXV, 777-778.

[12] "Si qui vero clerici seu monachi inventi fuerint coniurantes aut conspirantes, aut fratrias vel factiones componentes aliquas suis episcopis aut aliis, omnimodo cadant de proprio gradu."—C. 21, C. XI, q. 1.

[13] Council of Montpellier (1215), cap. XLV: "Quia propter coniurationes et conspirationes quae confratriae vocantur in civitatibus, villis, et castris, quandoque multa discordiae materia suscitatur: praesens synodus sub anathematis interminatione constituit, ut . . . non fiant de cetero confratriae, nisi de volun-

and approve the statutes [14] and to receive a report of the income together with the purpose for which it was used.[15]

These prescriptions gave to the ordinaries positive means for controlling these societies. Not numerous in themselves, these prescriptions nevertheless can be considered important in that they illustrate a period of transition. The Church previously had control over such societies only in so far as they acted either contrary to her laws or to the detriment of the spiritual welfare of the members. But by taking an active interest in these societies and by legislating in a positive manner the Church ushered in a new period of development in the history of societies.

B. *The Constitution "Quaecumque"*

The most important of the pertinent legislation of the Middle Ages is contained in the Constitution *"Quaecumque"* of Clement VIII, published December 7, 1604.[16] This Constitution made no reference to the establishment of confraternities by bishops, but legislated only concerning the form to be used by the orders of regulars, by religious institutes, by archconfraternities, and by congregations.[17] Hence the prescriptions it contained did not bind bishops.[18] Neither did they affect directly the private lay societies. However, the Constitution marks an important step in the Church's effort to control all religious societies, to root out abuses, and to direct them into religious lines. Hence certain portions of this Constitution will be cited here.

tate dominorum locorum ipsorum, et diocesani episcopi propter evidentem utilitatem id fiat."—Mansi, XXII, 949. Cf. also C. 21, C. XI, q. 1; Council of Sens (1528)—Mansi, XXXII, 1196.

[14] Provincial Council of Sens (1528)—*Loc. cit.*

[15] *Loc. cit.*

[16] *Fontes*, n. 192; *Bull. Rom.*, XI, 138-143.

[17] § 1: ". . . Regularium Ordinum, Religionum et institutorum . . . necnon Archconfraternitatum et Congregationum. . . ."—*Fontes*, n. 192.

[18] In the last century the Sacred Congregation of Indulgences issued several decrees deciding that when confraternities were founded by bishops, whether in virtue of ordinary or of delegated power, any authentic decree of the bishop was sufficient for validity.—S. C. Indulg., 25 ian. 1842, ad 4—*Decr. Auth.*, n. 298; 22 aug. 1842, ad 2—*Op. cit.*, n. 308; 22 aug. 1842, ad 1—*Op. cit.*, n. 312.

(a) In each city, town, or locality only one confraternity of a certain title was to be established and this with the consent of the ordinary.[19]

(b) When a new confraternity was to be established its statutes had to be approved by the bishop.[20]

(c) The officials of confraternities were in the matter of collecting alms and other offerings to obtain the required authorization from the bishop of the place where the collection was to be made. The bishop was to determine the manner in which the collection was to be made, but the Constitution expressly forbade the use of coin boxes or money tables.[21]

(d) Alms were to be used for the repair of churches or oratories or for other similar pious causes.[22]

(e) All confraternities and societies were to be established in accordance with the prescriptions of this Constitution, and all already exiting confraternities were to adopt them within a certain prescribed time.[23]

The other rules of the Constitution concerned mostly the aggregation of confraternities, the communication of privileges, and the sharing of indulgences.

After the Constitution *"Quaecumque"* legislation was frequently enacted in confirmation of its laws. Paul V published the Constitution *"Quae salubriter,"* in which he pronounced that societies were to follow the prescriptions of Clement's Constitution.[24] Some councils reiterated this legislation.[25] And the Sacred Congregation of

[19] § 2—*Fontes,* n. 192. Later legislation defined the size which was required of a city before more than one confraternity of the same nature could be established, and also the manner of measuring the required distance from the seat of administration of an already extant society before a society of identical character could be erected. The present law in this regard applies to Confraternities, the distance between which is left to the judgment of the Ordinary of the place. Cf. canon 711, § 1.

[20] § 5—*Loc. cit.*

[21] § 8: ". . . remotis tamen mensis pelvibus, et capsis. . . ."—*Loc. cit.*

[22] § 8—*Loc. cit.*

[23] This time was fixed at one year in Europe and two years elsewhere. Cf. § 10—*Loc. cit.*

[24] Paul V, const. *"Quae salubriter,"* 3 nov. 1610—*Fontes,* n. 196.

[25] Synod of Benevento (1693), tit. XXXI—*Acta et Decreta Conciliorum*

Indulgences in a general decree of January 8, 1861, insisted upon those societies which were included under the Constitution to follow its prescriptions.[26] Indeed, the Constitution *"Quaecumque"* remained the basic law of the Church on confraternities until the time of the Code.[27] However, certain exceptions were made to conform to the circumstances of the times or to give special encouragement to a certain kind of work or devotion, thus giving more freedom to the establishment of new societies.

After the issuance of the Constitution *"Quaecumque"* the Marians, directed especially by the Jesuits, were declared exempt.[28] All of the confraternities which had been established before the time of the Constitution were allowed to exist even though the requirement as to city or locality was not present, provided, however, that all the other prescriptions were followed. For those confraternities concerning the legality of which there was any doubt, which doubt in turn involved uncertainty concerning the validity of the annexed indulgences, Pius IX granted a sanation and ordered in the future that all the prescriptions were to be followed.[29]

Relative to those confraternities which were established after the issuance of the *"Quaecumque"* the law which permitted only one society of the same nature to be established in the same city was defined by authors as implying that another society of the same nature could not be locally established within a walking distance of one hour, or within a radius of three miles.[30] Nevertheless the privi-

Recentiorum, Collectio Lacensis (7 vols., Frieburgi Brisgoviae, 1870-1890), I, 61-62. Hereafter this collection of the Councils will be cited *Coll. Lac.* Cf. also Provincial Council of Rome (1725), Appendix XXII—*Coll. Lac.*, I, 446-447; Provincial Council of Prague (1860), tit. VI, cap. VII—*Coll. Lac.*, V, 562 a.

[26] *Fontes*, n. 5061.

[27] Beringer-Steinen, *Die Ablässe*, II, p. 12, n. 37. Besides being the basic law on confraternities until the Code, a great portion of it was incorporated into the Code.

[28] S. C. Indulg., *Societatis Jesu*, 29 aug. 1864—*Decr. Auth.*, n. 413; Beringer-Steinen, *Die Ablässe*, II, 193.

[29] S. C. Indulg., 19 oct. 1866—*Decr. Auth.*, n. 417; *Fontes*, n. 5074. In connection with this sanation the Sacred Congregation issued formulas to be observed in the erection and the aggregation of confraternities.—*Decr. Auth.*, Appendix XII-XIII.

[30] Beringer-Steinen, *Die Ablässe*, II, 22.

lege of exemption from this requirement was granted to some confraternities. Thus the Confraternities of Christian Doctrine and of the Blessed Sacrament both subsequently received this privilege,[31] as did also the Confraternity of the Blessed Virgin, established under the title of the Immaculate Conception, the members of which Confraternity were known as the "Children of Mary." [32]

C. *Later Legislation*

Later legislation was concerned to a great extent with the aggregation of confraternities [33] and the communication of indulgences,[34] and hence affected rather the approved or ecclesiastical societies. However, there was some legislation of note in a few isolated instances. The Council of Benevento (1693) did little more than repeat the Clementine Constitution.[35] But a council held at the same place five years later declared that all confraternities erected in the archdiocese before 1604 were invalid in their constitution, and further declared that all elections were invalid unless the names of the voting members were enrolled in a book for that purpose.[36] The Provincial Council of Naples in 1699 required the consent of the ordinary for the erection of new confraternities and enacted some prohibitions in relation to the transaction of business with close relatives by forbidding members to buy from or sell to those who were related to them within the second degree of consanguinity.[37] It also forbade

[31] S. C. Indulg., 23 apr. 1676—*Decr. Auth.*, n. 13; *Fontes,* n. 4948; 12 iul. 1847, ad 2—*Decr. Auth.*, n. 343; *Fontes,* n. 5042.

[32] S. C. Indulg., 30 aug. 1866—*Fontes,* n. 5073.

[33] S. C. Indulg., *Engolismen.*, 3 dec. 1892—*Fontes,* n. 5116; *ASS,* XXV (1892-1893), 427-429; 8 maii 1901—*ASS,* XXXV (1902-1903), 574; S. C. C., *Leopoliensem,* 10 nov. 1910, ad 1—*ASS,* III (1911), 390.

[34] S. C. C., *Leopolien.*, 10 nov. 1910, ad 2—*ASS,* III (1911), 390. For earlier legislation cf. S. C. Indulg., *Cameracen.*, 29 ian. 1720—*Decr. Auth.*, n. 74; S. C. Indulg., *Cameracen.*, 25 ian. 1842, ad 2—*Decr. Auth.*, n. 298—*Fontes,* n. 5022; *Briocen.*, 15 mart. 1852—*Decr. Auth.*, n. 358—*Fontes,* n. 5048; *Cameracen.*, 25 febr. 1877—*Decr. Auth.*, n. 431—*Fontes,* n. 5080.

[35] Tit. XXXI—*Coll. Lac.*, I, 61-62.

[36] Tit. VI—*Coll. Lac.*, I, 134.

[37] Tit. V, cap. IX, n. 3—*Coll. Lac.*, I, 204.

the holding of any office for a period of time longer than one year except by permission of the ordinary.[38]

In the year 1725 the Provincial Council of Rome called attention to the obligation of bishops to make visitations relative to the societies in their territories.[39] In the same year the Provincial Council of Avignon called attention to the many abuses that had crept into the various societies, such as the wasting of funds on banquets and other revelings,[40] and commanded a report to be made annually to the pastor as the special delegate of the bishop.[41]

The first legislation which entailed a universal application was enacted at the Council of Trent. Yet, though general or universal in application, it was not extensive in matter. Only two general rules were made. The first gave to the bishops the right of visiting the confraternities of the laity, not, however, without the permission of the king when the confraternity existed under the immediate royal protection.[42] The second law obliged all administrators of confraternities, both ecclesiastical and lay, to give a yearly report to the ordinary.[43] By their very nature these laws, though restricted in number, were important both because of their universal character and because of their effects. They gave the bishop at least some control over confraternities by his visitations, and enabled him to prevent abuses in view of the fact that there had to be rendered to him an account of all the expenditures.

D. *Particular Legislation in the United States of America*

Societies increased rapidly in the United States of America. This was due in part to the fact that many societies had already been

[38] *Loc. cit.*

[39] Tit. XXIII, cap. I—*Coll. Lac.*, I, 385. A complete summary of the legislation of the *"Quaecumque"* is given in an appendix to the enactments of this Council.—Appendix XXII—*Coll. Lac.*, V, 462.

[40] Tit. XL, Proemium—*Coll. Lac.*, I, 560.

[41] Tit. XL, cap. III—*Coll. Lac.*, I, 561.

[42] "Episcopi . . . habent ius visitandi . . . confraternitates laicorum . . . ; non tamen quae sub regum immediata protectione sunt, sine eorum licentia. . . ." —Sess. XXII, *de ref.*, c. 8.

[43] "Administratores, tam ecclesiastici, quam laici fabricae cuiusvis . . . confraternitatis . . . singulis annis teneantur reddere rationem administrationis ordinario. . . ."—Sess. XXII, *de ref.*, c. 9.

approved by the Church, some of which, as will be seen, were to be erected in every parish. However, many more sprang into existence. Legislation on societies centered principally around the Plenary Councils of Baltimore. However, prior to this time the Bishops of the United States in a letter addressed to the clergy in 1810 warned the faithful about joining secret societies, and reminded the priests that they were to refuse the sacraments to members of such societies.[44] At the I Provincial Council of Baltimore (1829) a Catholic Tract Society was formed and was to be incorporated under the laws of Maryland. This Society was formed for the purpose of disseminating books and pamphlets on Catholic doctrine and on the history of the Church in order to counteract the numerous anti-Catholic publications.[45] The IV Provincial Council of Baltimore was held in 1840. This Council ordered that the sacraments be refused to members of secret societies and also to members of those societies which encouraged excessive drinking. In turn the Council encouraged the establishment of temperance unions and sodalities in every parish.[46] The II Diocesan Synod of New Orleans (1844) went so far as to refuse Christian burial to members of secret societies.[47] Although this law did not concern lay societies, it did show the watchfulness which the Church exercised over all societies. More pertinent and of particular interest is a decree of the II Provincial Council of Cincinnati in 1858. It called attention to the numerous societies that existed among the youth of the province and expressed the desire to see established those societies which could be called strictly pious societies, or which had already been approved by the Holy See; others were not to be abolished, but their members were to be exhorted to pious and devotional practices.[48]

The I Plenary Council of Baltimore (1852) said very little about societies. It did, however, issue praise to those societies which were

[44] *Concilia Provincialia Baltimori habita ab anno 1829 usque ad annum 1849* (2. ed., Baltimori: Joannis Murphy et Socii, 1851), p. 28.

[45] Guilday, *A History of the Councils of Baltimore* (New York: The Macmillan Company, 1932), p. 95.

[46] *Concilia Provincialia Baltimori habita*, p. 172; Guilday, *op. cit.*, p. 125.

[47] Guilday, *op. cit.*, p. 146.

[48] Decr. X—*Coll. Lac.*, III, 210.

friendly to the Catholic youth.[49] The II Plenary Council of Baltimore (1866) issued some very special and pertinent legislation regarding lay societies. It recommended principally those societies which tended directly to preserve or to increase piety, and then presented an extensive list of approved societies.[50] Because of the great number and diverse forms of pious societies certain regulations were laid down in regard to the establishment of new societies:

(a) New societies were not to be instituted if the old ones already existing sufficed.

(b) A priest was not to institute a new society unless he had received the permission of the bishop in writing.

(c) If it became necessary to institute new societies, the regulations and practices of the previously existing societies were to be retained and followed as far as possible.

(d) No new society was to be approved by the bishop unless it was certain that it was entirely Catholic, both in its aims and in the laws by which it was to be governed, and that it was absolutely subject to the canonical authority of the bishop.[51]

The III Plenary Council of Baltimore (1884) legislated chiefly against forbidden societies. As its guide in this matter it appealed to the Encyclical Letter *"Humanum Genus"* of Leo XIII, which had been published on April 20th of the same year.[52] However, it also legislated on licit societies. The Council recommended the establishment of lawful societies, especially of those which were composed of working men, who, though they sought in part temporal and material ends, were to be under the direction of the clergy.[53]

[49] *Concilium Plenarium Totius Americae Septentrionalis Foederatae, Baltimori Habitum anno 1852* (Baltimori: Joannis Murphy et Socii, 1853), p. 13.

[50] "Cum ultimus Ecclesiae finis sit salus animarum, fovere debent sacerdotes illas praecipue Confraternitates, quae pietati conservandae vel augendae directe conducunt. . . ."—*Concilii Plenarii Baltimorensis II Acta et Decreta* (1866), n. 478.

[51] *Ibid.*, n. 480.

[52] *Acta et Decreta Concilii Baltimorensis Tertii A. D. MDCCCLXXXIV* (Baltimorae: Typis Joannis Murphy et Sociorum, 1886), n. 256. The text of the papal encyclical is contained in the *Fontes*, n. 591. Relative to forbidden societies there was also the Instruction of the Holy Office under date of May 10, 1884—*Fontes*, n. 1085; III Balt., *Appendix*, pp. 282-286.

[53] *Acta et Decreta*, n. 256. This same thought was later expressed in the

The Council furthermore ordered that in every parish or mission where the number of young people was sufficiently large for the purpose special societies were to be instituted for them,[54] and it gave special recommendation to such societies as the St. Vincent de Paul Society,[55] the Society for the Propagation of the Faith, and the various temperance societies that flourished at that time.[56]

E. *Ecclesiastical Recommendations*

That the Church has always approved of societies which furthered the interests of the Catholic religion, even if such were private lay societies, cannot be denied. No society that had a purely religious end was ever condemned, provided, of course, that it was not heretical and that it had no heretical tendencies. Even those which were not purely religious were often tolerated, as is evident from the condemnation merely of the abuses in the society rather than of the society itself. The latter means was employed only as a last resort for correcting existing evils. On the other hand, the Church has always looked upon organized societies as an excellent means of warding off sin and of leading their members to the practice of virtue,[57] and as an efficacious agency in saving souls and in promoting the due honor and glory of God.[58] As a result there are numerous instances in the history of societies, especially in the later Middle Ages and also more recently, wherein different societies have been recommended and praised, and some of them have been formally approved and erected.

Paul III in his Constitution *"Dominus Noster,"* November 30, 1539, approved the Confraternity of the Blessed Sacrament,[59] and in

encyclical *"Rerum Novarum"* of Leo XIII issued on May 15, 1891—*Fontes*, n. 611.

[54] *Acta et Decreta*, n. 257.

[55] Pope Gregory XVI (1831-1846) had granted many indulgences to the St. Vincent de Paul Society. For a modern example of recommendation cf. S. C. C., *Corrienten.*, 13 nov. 1920—*AAS*, XIII (1921), 135-144, especially pp. 141 ff.

[56] *Acta et Decreta*, nn. 257; 259; 260-263.

[57] *Conc. Plen. Baltimor. II Acta et Decreta*, n. 477.

[58] Provincial Council of Urbino, Italy (1859), Decr. CCXVIII—*Coll. Lac.*, VI, 72.

[59] *Bull. Rom.*, VI, 275-280.

his Constitution *"Altitudo Divinae Providentiae,"* February 7, 1541, confirmed a confraternity which existed in Rome for the care of orphans.[60] Benedict XIV in the Bull *"Gloriosae Dominae,"* September 27, 1748, gave numerous privileges to the Marians and praised the erection of the Marian Congregation.[61] The Provincial Council of Ravenna (1855) ordered pastors to erect the Confraternities of Christian Doctrine and of the Holy Name, also those which honored the Blessed Virgin Mary, and even others if the glory of God and the welfare of souls demanded it.[62] Somewhat the same ruling was made in the Provincial Council of Urbino (1859), Italy, which prescribed that at least one society should be erected in every parish.[63] This was akin to the decree of the IV Provincial Council of Baltimore (1840), mentioned above, which encouraged the erection of a temperance society in every parish [64] and a decree of the III Plenary Council of Baltimore (1884), which encouraged the erection of societies of working men.[65]

The purpose of the Church's approval of societies is potently manifest from the decrees of the Council of Mount Lebanon (1736), which was celebrated by the Maronites. The Council indicated that members of pious societies ought to possess a higher degree of sanctity than the faithful in general.[66] By this was meant that in such a society the faithful had more opportunity of doing good and of practicing virtue, and as a result could and should reach a higher degree of sanctity. In Ireland the praiseworthy formation of religious societies was stressed in a decree of the Provincial Council of Cashel in 1853. It recommended that the faithful belong to those sodalities which promoted frequent Communion.[67] And in the United States of America the II Plenary Council of Baltimore (1866)

[60] *Bull. Rom.*, VI, 307-312.

[61] *Bullarii Romani Continuatio Summorum Pontificum* (19 vols., Prato, 1757-1883), II, *Benedicti XIV Bullarium* (1846), 428-430. Hereafter this collection will be cited as *Bull. Rom. Cont.*

[62] Pars I, cap. VIII—*Coll. Lac.*, VI, 208.

[63] *Coll. Lac.*, VI, 72.

[64] *Concilia Provincialia Baltimori habita*, p. 172.

[65] *Acta et Decreta*, n. 256.

[66] Pars IV, cap. IV, n. 1—*Coll. Lac.*, II, 388.

[67] Tit. III, *De Eucharistia—Coll. Lac.*, III, 834, b.

in its final decree concerning the erection of confraternities prescribed that, in order to encourage the faithful to join pious societies, certain means were to be used to attract them, as, for example, the celebration of their feasts with added solemnity and the concession to the members of a special place of honor in processions in accordance with the rubrics.[68]

These laws, prescriptions, or recommendations were not always of a general nature. Indeed, they were more often particular than general. However, the very fact that synods and councils discussed and legislated concerning societies showed that they attracted widespread interest. The Church, following the pattern of these synods and councils, realized the value of the work accomplished by groups of the faithful united together to accomplish the works of piety and of charity for the welfare of their souls and the honor and glory of God.

Article 3. The Threefold Development of Lay Societies

A lay society in the Church is any union of the faithful, under properly constituted leadership, to attain some even though partial religious end. Such an end may consist in the increase of divine worship, or in the accomplishment of some work of piety or of charity. The former pertains directly to the honor of God, while the latter pertains to one's personal welfare and sanctity or to that of one's neighbor. From the concept of lay societies any society which has been erected or formally approved by the Church is excluded. The term includes only those societies which are governed and directed by the laity, even though as societies they stand commended, and even though they be constituted organically, or are of a universal or general character.

The first idea of a Christian religious society came with the foundation of Christ's Church. The Church itself was a society distinct from the State, perfect and independent, teaching a new freedom to man, and establishing an equal citizenship for all. Necessitated by the persecutions, the citizens of Christ's new social order congregated or met in the catacombs and other secret places to

[68] *Conc. Plen. Baltimor. II Acta et Decreta*, n. 482.

carry on divine services. Even though it may seem logical to expect it, yet there is no evidence to support the theory that societies for such an aim or purpose existed at a time prior to the persecutions. On the other hand, to trace medieval societies to their origin leads to the recognition of the earlier existence of two distinct kinds of societies, the purgatorial societies or the confraternities of prayer on the one hand, which could easily have had their origin in the early burial societies, and on the other hand the gilds.

Because there was no universal legislation concerning these societies before the time of the Council of Trent (1545-1563), it is impossible to distinguish clearly in all cases between ecclesiastical and lay societies up to the time of this Council. Even the Council itself made no perfectly clear distinction of this nature. Some societies were approved, but only after they had been instituted. Hence for such societies there was no such distinction at the time when they came into existence.

The confraternities of prayer arose among the clergy, a fact that does seem to distinguish them from the earlier burial societies. Later the laity were admitted. To the original purpose of praying for the dead, especially through the offering of Masses, other works of piety and charity were added. And though references to them are not copious or plentiful, it is not difficult to trace their development, at least till the Middle Ages, when they became more or less identified with the gilds.

Evidence of early gilds is more plentiful, but it cannot be accurately determined just when they actually assumed a religious character. Formed at first, even in the period belonging to ancient history, for temporal ends, the gilds by the early Middle Ages became primarily religious in character. The distinguishing feature of the gilds was the regular payment of dues, and, although they flourished longer in their specific features than the confraternities of prayer as distinct religious societies, yet by the beginning of the seventeenth century they, too, had disappeared.

Medieval societies may be considered as manifesting a combination of the features of the confraternities of prayer and of the gilds. Because these societies had a religious purpose in view, the Church endeavored to keep them faithful to it. At the same time the Church condemned the current abuses and ultimately sought in a positive way to direct and guide such groups. Consequently the legislation which the Church did enact was at first particular and prohibitive. The various prohibitions, although enacted at different times and even in different places, were gathered together and considered conjointly in order to prevent unnecessary repetition, to obtain a clearer idea of the prohibition in general, and to compare them more readily with similar demands to be met by the present law.

The same method was followed in the investigation of the positive legislation of the Church. It was noted that much of this positive legislation reflected the same character as the prohibitive measures which the Church invoked to wipe out abuses, except that it was stated in positive language. An exception to this was the Constitution *"Quaecumque"* in view of its comprehensive legislation and universal application. A great portion of it has become incorporated in the present Code of Canon Law.

But because the Constitution *"Quaecumque"* legislated mainly regarding ecclesiastical societies, although such a distinction was not clearly defined or recognized then, much of the legislation which was enacted later is also adduced, particularly the legislation of the II and III Plenary Councils of Baltimore. Such legislation for the greater part confirmed the prescriptions of the Clementine Constitution. However, some exceptions were made, especially with regard to those societies which were recommended or approved by the Church, and which the Church considered to be of greater importance and of more profound benefit.

Modern lay societies may be considered as having passed through a threefold stage of development. The initial stage is reflected in the origin within the Church of societies which proposed to themselves the accomplishment of some particular religious aim. They began as private groups without any ecclesiastical authorization. The members were joined loosely and possessed no hierarchical organization, but they did set for themselves the accomplishment of a truly religious purpose.

The next stage is manifested when the societies took on a truly organic character in view of a true hierarchical organization. This was probably due to some extent at least, to the influence of the gilds upon the confraternities of prayer, and from the fact that the gilds themselves became societies which professed a strictly religious aim. However, much of their religious character was lost in the course of time. This fact occasioned the repeated condemnations of the Church, which in turn paved the way for legislation of a more positive character. Thus the Church succeeded in gaining the necessary control whereby the undesirable societies could ultimately become eradicated for lack of all ecclesiastical commendation, and the commendable societies could become more firmly established. The Church's unerring recognition of true values as manifested in the existing societies paved the way for that commendation and approval which eventually crystallized in the Church's enactments that called for the establishment of certain universally obligatory societies.

The final stage of development appears in the circumstance that the Church did not exclude entirely those societies which she did not *formally* approve. Certain ones were *formally* condemned. At the same time, however, the Church often recommended or praised some societies which were not *formally* erected or approved. These were the lay societies in the strict sense. The Church's only concern was that such societies remain free from abuses and retain a religious end. Thus lay societies received at least an implicit ecclesiastical approval, which not only justified, but even recommended, their formation and continued existence for the achievement of religious ends and purposes among the laity, to whom as well as to the clergy has gone forth the apostolic call for Catholic Action.

CHAPTER IV

THE ESTABLISHMENT OF PARISH SOCIETIES

ARTICLE 1. THE MEANING OF THE TERM *Parish Society*

IT is not necesary to go again into the definition and meaning of a society. However, it will prove useful to clarify the term *parish society,* which in reality, or at least in effect, is identical with the term *lay society.* It is not the purpose of the present study to offer an explanation of the origin and development of the parish. A definition will suffice in the present treatise. A parish is a "gathering of the faithful living within a territory marked off by well defined limits over whom a proper priest is placed to exercise the care of souls.[1] The essential elements of a parish are a group of the faithful determined by a definite territory and directed by a specified priest. The concept of the parish has developed into that of an ecclesiastical entity. Its members are determined by strict territorial limits. Its pastor has the care of souls of all who live within these boundaries.[2] It is not difficult to conclude, then, that each one of the faithful should receive those things to which he has a right, namely, spiritual goods and all necessary help to salvation,[3] first of all from his pastor to whom the Church has committed his care. It but follows, then, that the parish has developed into a territorial unit within the Church, which unit should be the center of all spiritual or religious activity for the layman. There are exceptions, of course, but ordinarily works of piety and charity as well as any other public act of devotion should center around the parish. Societies should operate or function in conjunction with or as parish activities,[4] even

[1] Coady, *The Appointment of Pastors,* The Catholic University of America Canon Law Studies, n. 52 (Washington, D. C.: The Catholic University of America Press, 1929), p. 62. Cf. also canon 216, § 1; Fanfani, *De Iure Parochorum* (2. ed., Taurini-Romae, 1924), p. 2.

[2] Canon 451. This does not include non-baptized persons. Cf. canon 87.

[3] Canon 682.

[4] Cf. Garesché, *Modern Parish Problems* (New York: Joseph F. Wagner, Inc., 1928).

though the scope of the society reach beyond the limits of the parish. And though these activities are not confined to any particular parish, they are still considered parochial activities. Therefore in popular language lay societies are called parish societies. This terminology is preserved to emphasize the parish as the center of all activities of the lay society.

Article 2. The Right to Establish Parish Societies

Probably one of the best recommendations that can be given to parish societies is the fact that they have found their origin in the good will of the laity. In other words, they are a free expression of the will of the laity to co-operate in works of charity and piety, thus emphasizing the desire of the faithful to take an active part in the spread of Christ's teachings. This does not exclude the part which the clergy may have had in the origin of the societies. Their part was essential, it is true, but not official. Their part in the origin and development of the societies was exercised by them as private individuals, and not as clerics deputed with special power and authority over lay persons. Hence credit cannot be denied the laity in this respect.

Besides the many recommendations given to the various societies in the past [5] the Code recommends that the faithful [6] belong to those societies or associations which have been erected or at least commended by the Church.[7] Herein is implied the distinction between ecclesiastical and lay societies. Those which were commended or praised embrace some of the latter. The Code also implies a further distinction between formal erection [8] and approval.[9] A society is erected formally if the ordinary himself is the founder or issues the decree of erection thereby constituting

[5] Cf. *supra*, pp. 27-29.

[6] Under the name of the faithful are included both the clergy and the laity. Cf. canon 693, § 4.

[7] Canon 684: "Fideles laude digni sunt, si sua dent nomina associationibus ab Ecclesia erectis vel saltem commendatis. . . ."

[8] Canons 684; 686, § 1; 687; 708; etc.

[9] Canon 686, § 1.

it as an ecclesiastical moral person.[10] If some person inferior to the ordinary founds a society and the ordinary gives approval, that society becomes ecclesiastical in character but does not thereby become an ecclesiastical moral person. However, mere commendation or praise does not constitute formal approval, and hence does not change its lay character.[11]

There is some dispute upon just what constitutes formal approval and how it differs from mere recommendation or praise. Substantially the formula of approbation does not seem to differ from the formula of commendation. There is nothing to disprove that both can be given orally,[12] as well as in writing.[13] In some cases the approval or mere commendation can be determined from the context of the rescript or letter directed to the association or society. When this is not clear, then certain principles can be applied as an aid in determining whether the commendation constitutes formal approval. For former approval there is required:

(a) The express consent of the competent ecclesiastical authority.[14] This authority is the ordinary of the place. No one below an ordinary has this right unless he has received it by a special privilege.

(b) The express consent for each single society unit which is erected in different places.[15] A bishop could not approve a society erected in another diocese. Nor would his approval of a society in one parish constitute approval for the establishment of the same kind of society in another parish in his diocese.

On the other hand a society may be considered as commended only, and not as formally approved if a favorable testimonial is given:

[10] Canon 687. Cf. Wernz-Vidal, *Ius Canonicum* (7 vols. in 8, Romae: apud Aedes Universitatis Gregorianae, 1927-1938), III (1933), 507. This decree of erection is required for the erection of confraternities. Cf. canon 708.

[11] Schaefer, *De Religiosis*, n. 617.

[12] The approval for the erection of an ecclesiastical society can be given orally, but an ecclesiastical society cannot be formed into a juridic moral person except by a written decree of erection. Cf. canon 687.

[13] Beringer-Steinen, *Die Ablässe*, II, 41.

[14] De Meester, *Juris Canonici et Juris Canonico-Civilis Compendium* (3 vols. in 4, Brugis: Desclée, De Brouwer & Si, 1921-1928), II (1923), n. 1075.

[15] Vromant, *De Fidelium Associationibus* (Louvain: Museum Lessianum, 1932), p. 5, footnote 3.

(a) In general terms, *i. e.*, in a general way to the scope of the society, or to the purpose for which it was instituted, rather than to the society itself.

(b) Independently of any particular unit existing in a particular place under the same title, *i. e.*, without any direct intervention of ecclesiastical authority or any formal renewal of commendation.[16] This holds even in regard to the Confraternity of the Blessed Sacrament and the Confraternity of Christian Doctrine, the only two confraternities which the Code orders to be established in every parish.[17] As long as the ordinary's testimonial has been simply one of commendation, and not one of authoritative approval, the societies remain lay in character.

There are many societies extant today which have as yet received no ecclesiastical recommendation. However this does not militate against the possibility of the Church's ultimate approval. It merely emphasizes the Church's warning to the faithful to avoid those societies which are condemned or illicit.[18] It must not be forgotten that many societies sprang up without the intervention of ecclesiastical authority in any way, and later received the commendation or even the approval of the Church. Yet, in order to exclude with a sense of security all membership in any seditious society, the Church seems to discourage the erection of any new society which has not at least received a commendation from the local ordinary. This is but wise. It is the mind of the Church that no new society be founded so long as the existing ones are sufficient to care for the needs of the parish. However, if the laudable object of some new society is not fulfilled in the societies already existing, then the Church can well recommend that society's establishment and consider the founders as worthy of praise.

Some difficulty may be experienced in regard to the law of the Code which states that in no church is there recognized any society or association which has not been erected or at least approved by legitimate ecclesiastical authority.[19] This would seem to exclude

[16] *Loc. cit.* A renewal of commendation may, but not necessarily, does imply approval.

[17] Canon 711, § 2.

[18] Canon 684. Cf. *infra*, pp. 47-48.

[19] Canon 686, § 1.

the private institution of lay societies. However, by recognition here is meant the official recognition which implies the society's formal erection or at least its approval. The lack of this kind of recognition does not necessarily imply the absence also of commendation. If that were so, then canon 686, § 1, would involve a flat contradiction of canon 684 which recommends the faithful for joining associations or societies that stand even simply commended in the Church. The effect of the lack of *official* recognition for the societies founded by the laity is that it frees the Church from any specific responsibility in as far as their actions as a society are concerned. But it does not constitute a prohibition in their regard. This is evident from the constant practice of the Church in both commending and sometimes approving societies of this nature. It can therefore be licit and even praiseworthy for the faithful to join, or also to found, such societies, provided that there are observed in them those things which are required by the common law:[20]

The right to establish or to found societies is a natural right given to man by the law of nature.[21] This right is based upon the fact that man is a social being. As a general rule, what a man has a right to do himself he has a right to do with the help of others. There are many things which a man cannot do alone; other things can be done better with the help of others. "The experience of his own weakness urges man to call in help from without." [22] This is affirmed by Holy Scripture: "It is better therefore that two should be together than one; for they have the advantage of their society. If one fall he shall be supported by the other." [23] The right, then, of forming societies belongs to man by nature and cannot be denied him so long as the end for which he joins with others is good. And one's own sanctification, or also the promotion of works of piety and of charity is an end which is good in itself.

[20] De Meester, *Juris Canonici Compendium*, II, n. 1074.

[21] "Hac homo propensione naturali sicut ad coniunctionem ducitur congregationemque civilem, sic et alias cum civibus inire societates expetit, exiguas illas quidem nec perfectas, sed societates tamen."—Leo XIII, litt. encycl. *"Rerum Novarum,"* 15 maii 1891, n. 35—*Fontes*, n. 611.

[22] *"Rerum Novarum,"* n. 35—Authorized translation, The Paulist Press, 1939.

[23] Eccles. IV, 9-10.

ARTICLE 3. WHO HAS THE RIGHT TO ESTABLISH PARISH SOCIETIES?

Any person who has reached the age of majority [24] has the right to form a parish society.[25] Since minors in the exercise of their rights are subject to their parents or guardians, except in those things in which they are expressly exempt by law,[26] they have no right to form societies. And even adults who have this right by the law of nature are restricted somewhat in its use. These restrictions will be discussed under the treatment regarding both the object of societies [27] and the rights of the pastor and the ordinary concerning them.[28] In a word, as long as the end of the society is good and does not infringe upon the rights of the pastor or of the ordinary the right to found the society can be exercised. No approval is required. If the consent of the ordinary were required, as was formerly the case, the society would become ecclesiastical and thus lose its lay character. The Vicar General is excluded by law from erecting ecclesiastical societies without, at least, a general mandate.[29] However, this prohibition applies only to ecclesiastical societies and does not restrict the right of the Vicar General to organize a lay society. The same is true of any priest.

The prescripts of the II Plenary Council of Baltimore (1866), which forbade priests to form societies without the written permission of the bishop,[30] seemed to limit the right of a priest. In not making any distinction between ecclesiastical and lay societies the law apparently applied to all societies alike. However, this particular law could not have been enacted with a view to abrogating any of the general laws in existence at the time, nor did it mean to nullify any of the Church's recommendations regarding the institution of such societies which could prove useful to the spiritual welfare of

[24] Canon 88, § 1, identifies this age with the completion of 21 years of life.

[25] "Persona maior plenum habet suorum iurium exercitium."—Canon 89.

[26] Canon 89.

[27] The object of parish societies is treated in Article 5 in this Chapter.

[28] In Chapter VIII the rights of the pastor are treated under Article 2 and the rights of the ordinary are treated under Article 4.

[29] Canon 686, § 4.

[30] *Conc. Plen. Baltimor. II Acta et Decreta*, n. 480. Cf. *supra*, p. 26.

the faithful.[31] Furthermore, since there was no distinction between ecclesiastical and lay societies at that time, the Council simply legislated regarding societies as they then existed. With the advent of the Code such a distinction was made and useful lay societies now stand recommended, even though they be not officially approved by the Church. The recognition of this distinction by the Code seems to take much of the force from this conciliar law, especially in view of the fact that the Code praises membership in the simply recommended societies, which by their very nature have not been erected or approved by the bishop.[32]

The law of the Council can be considered to remain still in force merely in the form of an authoritative exhortation. The natural right of the priest to form societies can be exercised as long as other prescripts of the Council and of the law are not violated. Therefore, if the societies already existing are not sufficient, if the new society conforms as closely as possible to the approved societies, if it is Catholic in character, and if it remains subject to the authority of the Church [33] (not as an ecclesiastical association, but rather by way of subjection to the general vigilance of the Church), then a priest can found such a new society. It was the will of the Council that the bishop's permission be obtained. But such a permission would according to the present law of the Code imply the authoritative approval which suffices to characterize the newly formed society as an ecclesiastical society under the special supervision of the Church. Hence, if a new society is to retain the nature of a lay society in its formation, then it must be formed apart from the bishop's permission which the Council required. It thus becomes evident that a lay society can be established by a priest as long as the pious works which it intends to promote have merited the Church's simple recommendation.

A law which was often repeated in the past restricted the establishment of a new confraternity of the same title in the same place.[34]

[31] Cf. *supra*, pp. 27-28.

[32] Canon 684. Cf. *supra*, pp. 34-37.

[33] *Conc. Plen. Baltimor. II Acta et Decreta*, n. 480.

[34] Clement VIII, const. *"Quaecumque,"* 7 dec. 1604—*Fontes*, n. 192; S. C. Indulg., *Ordinis Praedicatorum*, 20 maii 1896, ad III—*ASS*, XXVIII (1895-

The purpose of this prohibition was not only the avoidance of confusion but also the prevention of harm to existing societies which would result if other units were allowed to be established in the same place. If the new societies were not of the same title with the existing ones, or if their purpose, or even the means used by them to attain the same end, was not identical with that of the already extant societies, then the formation of new societies did not fall under this prohibition.[35] The present law places this same restriction upon the formation of new confraternities and pious unions.[36] While this law does not involve lay societies, yet it can be also applied in their regard, especially in view of the prescript of the Council of Baltimore mentioned above, which forbade the erection of new societies if those already existing were sufficient. Not only would confusion result from a multiplication of the same society in the same parish or same place, but each individual unit would tend to weaken the other, so that it would be a detriment to the society itself in seeking its end as well as a hindrance to the individual members. Reason dictates that no society with the same end be formed in a place where a society of that nature already exists.[37]

Article 4. Incorporated and Non-Incorporated Societies

A. *In Canon Law*

A society may be formed as a moral person, that is, as a corporation, or it may be formed without this legal characteristic. A collegiate moral person implies a union of at least three physical

1896), 751—*Fontes,* n. 5127; S. C. Indulg., 14 sept. 1904—*ASS,* XXXVII (1904-1905), 394.

[35] Vromant, *De Fidelium Associationibus,* p. 89.

[36] Canon 711, § 1.

[37] An important decision was given by the Sacred Congregation of Indulgences which permitted the establishment of more than one confraternity in the same city if the size of the city, in the judgment of the ordinary, warranted it.—*Ordinis Praedicatorum,* 20 maii 1896, ad VI—*ASS,* XXVII (1895-1896), 751-752. On Sept. 14, 1904, the same Congregation decreed that the distance was to be computed from church to church and not from the limits of parish to parish.—*ASS,* XXXVII (1904-1905), 394.

persons [38] to which the Code grants various rights.[39] In Canon Law a moral person cannot be constituted except by public authority.[40] The right of existence in the capacity of a moral person is conceded either by the law itself or by a competent superior through a formal decree.[41] If a society is organized as a moral person it necessarily exists as an ecclesiastical association. For the erection of a moral person the law requires the written decree of a competent superior,[42] and thus a society, if it is erected by a written decree, becomes in virtue of the law itself an ecclesiastical society.[43] Therefore no parish society in its nature of a lay society can be erected as a moral person in Church law. However, in order to understand more clearly the legal status of parish societies it is necessary to have some understanding of the legal aspects of ecclesiastical corporations.

B. *In Civil Law*

There has been much discussion upon the exact legal status of ecclesiastical corporations. But their status is becoming more clearly defined especially in view of recent statutory law and court decisions.[44] An ecclesiastical corporation is now recognized as a legal corporation by the State. The civil law does not create these corporations but finds and accepts them as products of the social life.[45] This recognition or acceptation applies to "diocesan or parish corporations, and other religious aggregate entities." [46] Although these higher ecclesiastical corporations, *i. e.*, parishes, dioceses, etc., generally obtain a charter of incorporation from the State, yet in some States, this would not seem to be so much a necessity as a safeguard. For the recognition of the State, depending upon statutory

[38] Canon 100, § 1.

[39] Canons 100-102; 1489-1494.

[40] Canon 99.

[41] Canon 100, § 1.

[42] *Loc. cit.*

[43] Canon 687.

[44] White, "Certain Aspects of the Legal Status of the Church in the United States"—*The Jurist*, I (1941), 21.

[45] Blackstone-Cooley, *Commentary*, I, 472.

[46] White, *loc. cit.*

law in the individual States, may extend to the *corporation sole.*[47] This gives to religious corporations generally the same rights as any other form of corporation. For example, a New York court has declared that American religious corporations are "to be controlled and managed according to the principles of the common law as administered by the ordinary tribunals of justice." [48]

From this it cannot be concluded that religious corporations receive full recognition in common law. The principles of common law do not consider the ecclesiastical aspect of religious societies which, as a result, receive no legal recognition in so far as they are ecclesiastical.[49] But their legal or civil rights "will be on a perfect par with those of any other society which has obtained corporate existence." [50] Their sphere of activity is thus restricted to making contracts and acquiring, holding, and disposing of property,[51] without any recognization of their ecclesiastical status. "The corporation thus has neither public nor ecclesiastical functions, being a mere business agent with strictly private secular powers." [52]

However, somewhat more recently a distinction has arisen from the recognition of the two aspects of such corporations, the religious and the civil. "And even in the case of an unincorporated ecclesiastical organization civil jurists distinguish between the church and

[47] A *corporation sole* is one which is composed of a single member only and his successors.—Pomeroy, *Business Law* (Cincinnati: South-Western Publishing Co., 1931), p. 541; Zollman, *American Church Law* (St. Paul: West Publishing Co., 1933), n. 101. The III Plenary Council of Baltimore (1884), prescribed the *corporation sole* as one legal alternative in the administration of church property.—*Conc. Plen. Baltimor. III Acta et Decreta,* n. 266. However some States do not recognize the *corporation sole.*

[48] Robertson v. Bullions, 11 N. Y., 243, 251. Cf. also Zollman, *op. cit.,* § 126.

[49] White, *loc. cit.*

[50] Heston, *The Alienation of Church Property in the United States,* The Catholic University of America Canon Law Studies, n. 132 (Washington, D. C.: The Catholic University of America Press, 1941), p. 56.

[51] Zollman, *op. cit.,* § 147; Brown, *The Canonical Juristic Personality with Special Reference to Its Status in the United States of America* (Washington, 1927), pp. 121-130.

[52] Zollman, *op. cit.,* § 147.

the society." [53] In the eyes of the civil courts church societies are not necessarily composed of members of the church. What belongs to the spiritual realm falls under the jurisdiction of the Church, while the State has the exclusive rights over temporalities. In relation, then, to questions of faith and morals, or ecclesiastical discipline, the basic right of the Church is upheld by the courts.[54] This does not give corporations any more rights in so far as they are religious or ecclesiastical. It simply recognizes the jurisdiction of the Church in spiritual matters. In questions of temporalities, or in matters wherein the State claims jurisdiction, a decision will be rendered by the court according to civil law if the society is incorporated. If it is not incorporated, the court will leave religious matters to the Church, adjudge property matters by the civil law, and will decide other matters according to the internal laws of the organization itself provided they are not contrary to the State law.[55]

Therefore in the recognition of religious associations there can be distinguished a twofold stage of development. The first stage consisted of the acceptation by the courts of ecclesiastical entities as legal entities in regard to their civil rights without any recognition of their religious character. They were thereby placed on a par with civil corporations. The second stage consisted in the recognition of ecclesiastical jurisdiction in spiritual matters. While this recognition did not accord to societies any additional civil rights, it did constitute a step forward in the civil admission of the jurisdiction of the Church.

When the civil courts speak of religious societies and when they say they will look to the internal laws of unincorporated religious societies, they are referring to congregations, *i. e.*, the parish group

[53] Heston, *op. cit.*, p. 57.

[54] "Whenever the questions of discipline, faith, or ecclesiastical rule, custom or law have been decided by the highest of these church judicatories to which the matter has been carried, the legal tribunals must accept these decisions as final, and as binding in their application to the case before them."—Watson v. Jones, 80 U. S. (13 Wall), 679 and 727. There have, however, been some decisions contrary to this so-called "higher-plane theory," but Watson v. Jones is considered the leading case and has established precedent.

[55] Dockhus v. Lithuanian, 206 Pa. 25. This decision refers to parishes, etc., and not to societies within the parish.

as such and not to pious societies within the parish. Such groups, if unincorporated, would receive no recognition as societies; their sole rights would be resident in each member and all would have to sue by individual name.[56]

A lay society, therefore, enjoys the status of a legal entity only in so far as it is incorporated. What is not considered a moral person by the Church will also not be recognized as a corporation unless it be incorporated in civil law. Only in regard to parish congregations and higher ecclesiastical organizations will the courts leave spiritual matters to the Church, settle legal or property disputes according to the civil law, and other disputes according to the internal laws of the organization itself, provided that they are not contrary to the State law. A society, therefore, would be benefited by legal incorporation, especially if it possessed a large amount of property, personal or real.[57] However, it must not be forgotten that the legal title of property cannot rest in an unincorporated lay society. This will be explained later.[58] For the present it will suffice to say that most lay societies are of such a nature that incorporation is neither necessary nor practical, although their status is recognized in civil law to the extent that has here been indicated.

Article 5. Object of Parish Societies

A. *Recommended and Licit Ends*

(1) *Personal Sanctification:* The end or the purpose for which societies are established is identical both in regard to ecclesiastical societies and in regard to parish societies. As stated in the Code, this end embraces one's own personal sanctification, the exercise of works of piety and charity, or the enhancement of public worship.[59] One's personal sanctification must be one's first aim in life. Christ founded His Church to give to mankind the means of salvation.

[56] Zollman, n. 125.

[57] Charitable institutions, hospitals, etc., would more likely have occasion to have such possessions. But these institutions are not societies in the sense of parish societies.

[58] Cf. *infra*, pp. 77-78.

[59] Canon 685.

That, therefore, is the aim of the Church. It must be the aim of every pastor and, primarily, of every public activity carried on in the parish, and, consequently, of every society within the parish. Therefore a true parish society must have personal sanctification of the members as one of its objects and must consequently be able to afford some means to acquire this end.

Since all men are not of the same temperament or nature, but possess various likes and inclinations, it follows that not all men are attracted by the same things. It seems not only useful but necessary that there exist in the Church many religious orders to which access is had by all, but to which not all are called. Only a few are called to live a strict religious life, that is, a life in common under the observance of the evangelical counsels through the vows of obedience, chastity, and poverty.[60] Not many are called to observe the common life with solemn, simple, or temporary vows, or even without vows.[61] For those who live in the world, and yet wish to share something in common, the Church has permitted the institution of various kinds of societies. Because of the variety of societies it is not difficult for anyone to find one which appeals to his nature. Thus a society can be a means, over and above the ordinary means offered by the Church, of personal sanctification to those who wish to acquire a higher degree of sanctity.

(2) *Works of Piety and Charity:* The Church itself is sufficient for each one to acquire personal sanctification. However, it is known that not every individual does of himself attain this end. If the Church does not save all, certainly a society within the Church cannot do so. Yet it can be and often is the means of inducing not only those who belong to it, but also others, to higher degrees of sanctification through works of piety and charity. And because it can be a means of good towards others, there can be no doubt that a parish society is often the means of saving souls both by bringing new sheep into the fold besides reclaiming many of those who have strayed from it.

Not every society needs to have this particular purpose for its object. But if a group of the faithful form a society with this object

[60] Canon 487.

[61] For communities without vows cf. canons 673-681.

in mind, namely, to perform works of piety and charity towards others, it certainly is a sufficient object in itself. No specific acts of piety or charity are demanded. It may be interesting to note that the Provincial Council of Sens, France, in 1528, decreed that societies use their income for the repair of churches, the relief of the poor, or for other pious uses as the bishop saw fit.[62] Under present legislation nowhere is any specific use demanded of the income. Although such use is generally stated in the statutes, it may be left to the will of the society.

(3) *The Increase of Public Worship:* The third object of parish societies is the increase of public divine worship. This is the special object which all confraternities have according to the Code, since a confraternity is a sodality, or a corporation, erected for this special purpose.[63] This, however, does not exclude other societies from having the same purpose. Such a case could easily be verified in a parish society erected for the sake of promoting the honor of the patron of a parish. The parish of St. Henry, for example, could establish a society for the purpose of fostering devotion to St. Henry. Special services or devotions could be held in accordance with liturgical laws either within or outside of the church. Thus the society, while remaining a parish or lay society, would have as its primary purpose the enhancement of public worship alongside of the added purpose of personal sanctification.

(4) *Licit Temporal Ends:* As has been seen, societies were instituted by the laity mostly to attain some religious end. At times the Church has endeavored to make the end of these societies purely religious. However, no society of this nature was ever condemned, even though its end was not entirely religious, so long as it was not the cause or the occasion of abuse. Therefore there exist today certain beneficent societies, not entirely religious in purpose, yet having at least the implicit sanction of ecclesiastical authority.

The end of a society need not be entirely religious. It need not embrace all three of the above mentioned objects. It need not have one to the exclusion of the other two, nor to the exclusion of any

[62] Hardouin, IX, 1960-1961.

[63] Canon 707.

other good end. As long as the society has at least a partial religious end it can still be considered a parish society.[64]

This is no place to discuss the relative value of various societies. Perhaps a society with a purely religious end is of greater benefit in itself. Yet temporal goods should be an aid in seeking spiritual things, and a society may be of greater benefit to some individuals if it has besides a religious end also a temporal one.[65] This is not a point to be argued now. The fact remains that parish societies must have a religious end, but not exclusively so. It suffices that their end be at least partially religious.

B. *Illicit Ends Forbidden by Law*

Certain kinds of societies are forbidden because their purpose or object is evil. The faithful are especially warned and forbidden against joining such societies. Therefore it follows that no society which falls under this class can be established even as a private lay society.[66]

Secrecy, if it be insisted on to such an extent that the purpose of the society cannot be revealed to the ecclesiastical or civil authorities, is forbidden.[67] Any purpose contrary to the good of the Church must be excluded. Likewise any seditious intention, such as activity against the public order or the government, could not enter into a parish society. Anything contrary to faith and morals

[64] Coronata speaks of *associationes boni* whose end is mutual aid. These would not be parish societies unless they joined with their temporal end some spiritual end. Cf. Coronata, *Institutiones Iuris Canonici* (5 vols., Taurini, 1928-1936), II, n. 667.

[65] Leo XIII encouraged associations whose end was the bettering of the social life of working men. To this end was to be added a religious end also. This plainly was a society with both a temporal and a spiritual end. Cf. "*Rerum Novarum,*"—*Fontes,* n. 611.

[66] Fidales laude digni sunt, si sua dent nomina associationibus ab Ecclesia erectis vel saltem commendatis; caveant autem ab associationibus secretis, damnatis, seditiosis, suspectis aut quae studeant sese a legitima Ecclesiae vigilantia subducere.—Canon 684. Cf. also Schaefer, *De Religiosis,* pp. 1042-1043.

[67] Leo XIII, encycl. "*Rerum Novarum,*" 15 maii 1891—*Fontes,* n. 611; Pius XI, encycl. "*Quadragesimo Anno,*" 15 maii 1931—*AAS,* XXIII (1931), pp. 186-189; *Conc. Plenar. Baltimor. I Acta et Decreta* (1866), tit. XII, n. 511.

or anything that would be a danger to faith and morals, such as is found in the so-called suspected societies, would necessarily by its very nature be forbidden.[68] Finally, if the purpose of the society were such that it would flinch from the vigilance of the Church, even though it was not secret, such a status would give rise to suspicion.[69]

If any person had as his aim or purpose any of the above mentioned objects he would have no right to establish a society. The Church prohibits such a society from being formed. Otherwise, if the end were good and at least partially religious, the right to found a society could not be infringed upon.

[68] S. C. S. Off., *Epistola ad locorum Ordinarios, qua eorum vigilantia excitatur circa nova quaedam acatholicorum molimina contra fidem,* 5 nov. 1920—*AAS,* XII (1920), 595-597.

[69] Pius X, epistola encyclica, 15 nov. 1912—*AAS,* IV (1912), 657-662. Cf. also Schaefer, *De Religiosis,* pp. 1042-1043.

CHAPTER V

THE CONSTITUTION OF A SOCIETY

ALTHOUGH a society can be a union of a certain number of the laity only loosely united for the purpose of some end at least partially religious, still some sort of union is required. If a certain group assembled merely to perform some work of charity under the leadership of one or more, such an act could hardly be called the act of a society. There would have to be some sort of stability to that union. It would not have to be perpetual or indefinite as to time. Yet there would have to be some intention on the part of those forming the society to continue to act in unison for some time at least in the fulfillment of its end. A parallel might be drawn in the distinction between the virtue of charity and an act of charity. An act of charity is something done here and now out of love for one's neighbor. The virtue of charity is the continued practice or the habit of being charitable. Thus a society must be formed to pursue habitually some religious end. It is, therefore, best that it have some sort of constitution in order to have more stability in its union. The most important features of the constitution of a society are its title, statutes, meetings, and officers.

ARTICLE 1. TITLE

A title is not an essential element of a society. Yet it would be almost inconceivable for a society to have no title at all. No special title can be required of a lay society. Yet in regard to ecclesiastical societies, the law demands that they refrain from the use of titles which denote levity or novelty, or which indicate some kind of devotion not approved by the Holy See.[1] This can also be applied to lay societies because of the similar purpose which they serve. Furthermore, any title that is contrary to faith and morals is prohibited by its very nature.

[1] Canon 688.

Titles which are generally used and which are recommendable for lay societies are those which relate to the attributes of God, or the mysteries of religion, those which derive from the feasts of our Lord, of the Blessed Virgin or of the saints, and those which bespeak or describe the pious or charitable work of the society itself.[2] But other names or titles are also permissible. This includes also some titles which were prohibited in the past but which can now be used.[3] But it excludes titles that belong to other associations, either ecclesiastical or lay.

Article 2. Statutes

The Code distinguishes between statutes and special norms of associations.[4] Statutes comprise the fundamental constitution of a whole association which generally embraces or can embrace many particular units, which units as parts of the same society or association are equally bound by the same statutes.[5] Norms, on the other hand, are practical rules which are made by each individual unit, and bind only that particular unit by which they were made. In popular terms they are usually referred to as the by-laws of a society.

Prior to the time of the Code the privilege of not having statutes was granted to some societies.[6] However, the advantage of this is a little difficult to see. Furthermore, this privilege was not restated in the Code. The present law states that every association must have its own statutes, examined and approved by the Holy See or the ordinary of the place.[7] The same authority, therefore, is required to approve statutes as is required to approve, to form, or to

[2] Schaefer, *De Religiosis*, n. 619; Vromant, *De Fidelium Associationibus*, p. 20.

[3] An example of a title of this nature is: "The Eucharistic Heart of Jesus." Cf. S. R. C., *decretum*, 28 mar. 1914—*AAS*, VI (1914), 146; S. R. C., 15 iulii 1914—*AAS*, VI (1914), 382; S. R. C., 9 nov. 1921—*AAS*, XIII (1921), 545.

[4] Canons 697, § 1, and 715, § 1.

[5] Coronata, *Institutiones*, I, 908; Wernz-Vidal, *Ius Canonicum*, II, 511-512.

[6] Schaefer, *De Religiosis*, n. 620.

[7] Canon 689, § 1.

erect an ecclesiastical association.[8] This authority is required because the statutes regulate the nature and purpose of a society, the mode of organization, and the rights and duties of the members. These points are specifically mentioned for the sake of emphasizing their importance. Even though lay societies are not bound by this law of the Code, nevertheless utility, if not necessity, demands that in view of these important elements there be drawn up statutes and by-laws of some sort in order to preserve unity and stability, and to protect the various members. Statutes will safeguard the society if new branches of it are formed, while by-laws will contribute greatly to the preservation of order within the society itself.[9]

Article 3. Meetings

An important feature in the constitution of any society centers about the society's meetings. There is no obligation in regard to lay societies to hold regular meetings. The Code gives this right to ecclesiastical associations legitimately erected,[10] but this by no means excludes any other organization from using the same kind of right. One of the purposes of a meeting is to gain greater facility in attaining the end for which the society was founded. Without meetings not all the members would have an active part in the activities of the society. A society is a union of the faithful. That union designates not only a moral union but also a physical one whereby a number of the faithful can attain some spiritual end. Disunity would result from a lack of meetings.

Each member should have a voice in the election of officers.[11]

[8] Since a Vicar General cannot approve or erect ecclesiastical societies, he cannot, without a special mandate, approve the statutes of those societies which are erected with the status of a moral personality. Whether or not he can approve the statutes of those societies which are not erected with that specific status is doubtful. Cf. Coronata, *Institutiones,* I, n. 674; S. C. Indulg., *Aurelianen.,* 18 aug. 1868—*Decr. Auth.,* n. 420, ad 4.

[9] For a form of general statutes for confraternities cf. Pius XI, motu prop., "*De Pio Opera a Propagatione Fidei amplificanda,*" 3 maii 1922—*AAS,* XIV (1922), 321-330, in particular 326 ff.

[10] Canon 697.

[11] Sometimes certain classes of members are excluded from this right, *e. g.,* honorary members. This is no infringement of rights if the statutes limit this right.

It is also the right of each member to assist in determining the manner or the method in which the end of the society is to be attained. Other business, too, can be carried out at the meetings. Especially recommended are some educational or religious exercises, among which may be numbered "Discussion Clubs," which have proved to be very successful.

Foreign to the meetings as well as to the spirit of parish societies are many abuses that have been condemned in the past.[12] Probably the most prevalent of these abuses were occasioned by the use of intoxicating drinks at meetings, the discussion of dogmatic questions by lay persons, and, in general, the conducting of a meeting without the presence of a priest. There was nothing in any of the laws to indicate that some social activity during a meeting was ever forbidden. What was forbidden was excesses in these matters. However, experience has taught that activities of this kind can better be postponed till after the meeting. And there, too, moderation must be the rule, for excess in these matters soon obscures the real religious character of the society, induces some to become members for social reasons alone, and consequently hinders others in the fulfillment of the end of the society.

Article 4. Officers

Except for what the civil law may demand for an incorporated society, nowhere are there any specific demands regarding the number or kind of officers. The Code does speak, however, of a president and other officers,[13] and an administrator.[14] In collegiate societies also a secretary is mentioned in connection with the elections.[15] Besides the president, therefore, no specific officer is demanded. The proper demand must be determined, then, in the statutes or constitution of each society. Practically all societies follow parliamentary law in this regard. But any office may be added or omitted according to the needs of the society.

[12] Cf. *supra*, pp. 17-18.

[13] Canons 697, § 1, and 715, § 1. Cf. also canons 161-182.

[14] Canon 697, § 1.

[15] Canon 171, § 5.

Another point in regard to officers is the length of time for which they hold office. A practical law was enacted at the Provincial Council of Naples (1699), which made it illegal to hold an office for over a period of one year except by permission of the ordinary.[16] This is the custom adopted by most societies and is extremely practical in that it gives each one an opportunity to take a more active part in the affairs of the society. Its wisdom is confirmed by the Code, which limits the time of offices of religious superiors.[17] The length of time and the number of terms permitted should be determined in the statutes.

The question of officers is an important one in any society. Often success or failure depends upon leadership. For the election of a religious superior the Code states that it is matter of conscience for each one to choose him who according to his discreet judgment is worthy.[18] While the same rule does not apply so strictly for the election of officers in parish societies yet, though it may not be wrong to vote for some one who is less worthy, it is a matter of common sense to choose some one who is capable of successful leadership.

The method of choosing or electing the officers depends upon the will of the members. It is usually outlined in the statutes. For elections in ecclesiastical associations erected as moral personalities the method to be followed is the same as that which is laid down in the Code for observance by collegiate moral persons,[19] and proceeds according to the statutes as long as they are not contrary to these laws.[20] This legislation was evolved from the long practice of the Church. It may well be recommended for observance on the part of all parish societies in their weighty tasks of selecting competent officers.

16 Tit. V, Cap. IV, n. 3—*Coll. Lac.*, I, 204.

17 Canon 505.

18 Canon 506, § 1.

19 Canon 697, § 2. These laws are contained in canons 161-182.

20 Canon 697, § 2.

CHAPTER VI

THE MEMBERS

ARTICLE 1. QUALIFICATIONS FOR MEMBERSHIP

A. *Who Can Be Members?*

ALTHOUGH the linking of a parish society with a parish is not an essential feature of such a society, yet inasmuch as the society is considered as pertaining to and operating under the guidance or supervision of a given parish, it follows that any member of that parish to which the society is attached has the right to join such a society as long as he is not legitimately barred or impeded by the law from becoming a member. This right must be extended to minors who have reached the age of puberty. There is no specific law in the Code to confirm this statement but the Code does give to minors who have reached the age of puberty the right of answering for themselves in spiritual matters.[1] Although this law refers directly to judicial processes, yet there seems to be no reason militating against its application here. This right of minors to answer for themselves in spiritual matters is a special concession of the law in that, although minors "enjoy habitually or radically the same rights as those who are of age, they are nevertheless hampered in their enjoyment,"[2] because they are in most things subject to the power of their parents or guardians. It must be stressed that minors cannot form societies. The distinction between founding a society and merely joining one lies in the fact that the former is to a certain extent a juridic act not connected solely with one's own spiritual welfare, but affecting that of others also, for a society is a union of two or more persons. Joining an already existing society can relate purely to one's own spiritual welfare. This is substantiated

[1] Canon 1648, § 3. The law here does not distinguish between the sexes, but places the age at fourteen for both boys and girls.

[2] Augustine, *A Commentary on the New Code of Canon Law* (8 vols., St. Louis-London: B. Herder Book Co., 1930-1936), II (6. ed., 1936), 11.

by the common law of the Church. The law grants to those who have completed their fifteenth year of life the right to enter a novitiate,[3] for the choice of a state of life is a right which minors can exercise freely unless they are canonically impeded from it. For the same reason the canonical age which suffices for a person contracting marriage is not the age of majority but an appreciably younger age,[4] even though the Church makes it illicit for minors to marry as long as their parents are reasonably opposed to the marriage.[5] Joining a society can be likened, in a smaller degree, to entering a special state of life. A person joins in order that he may work in common with others and thus share with them some spiritual benefits. This right then cannot be denied to minors as long as it concerns purely spiritual matters. However, many other incidental questions can arise which would hinder minors from becoming members.

Some restriction, too, may be placed upon adults as well as upon minors in the matter of joining a society. Since a society is a free union formed voluntarily, even adults can be barred from gaining membership in such a free association. Potential members can be granted or refused admission in dependence upon the free will of the members.[6] Whether or not a candidate must be a member of the parish in which the society is located is another question. There is no law that demands this. Expediency may sometimes permit it. However, it can be stated as a general rule that a person should, if possible, be linked with some society in his own parish, and thus partake in the activities of his own parish. This, at least, is the spirit of the Church law.[7] The fact that a person belongs to another society or to many other societies does not constitute a reason for not admitting him, provided only that the society in which he seeks admission is not incompatible with any of the societies in which he is a member.[8]

[3] Canon 555, § 1, 1°.

[4] Canon 1067, § 1.

[5] Canon 1034.

[6] Generally the majority vote of the members is required for the granting of admission to membership. Cf. De Meester, *Juris Canonici Compendium,* II, 504.

[7] Cf. *supra,* pp. 33-34.

[8] Cf. canon 693, § 2.

B. *Who Cannot Be Admitted to Membership?*

Just as certain ends or objects must remain excluded from societies because they are forbidden by the Church,[9] so also certain classes of people must be barred from gaining membership in parish societies.[10] The following are forbidden by canon law from validly becoming members of approved ecclesiastical societies, and this prohibition by its very nature must be extended in most cases to all societies in the Church, even if these are only recommended, or even only recognized as licit societies within the Church.

1. *Non-Catholics.* Under this name come all the baptized who have defected from the faith (apostates), or who pertinaciously adhere to an erroneous doctrine or call it into positive doubt the while they still retain the name of Christian (heretics), or who repudiate their subjection to the supreme authority in the Church or in the practice of their religion refuse communication with the duly subject members of the Church (schismatics),[11] as well as all non-baptized persons (infidels).[12]

2. *Those Who Belong to a Condemned Sect.* Among these are to be included all members of any kind of an association that militates against the Church or legitimate civil authority,[13] even though it has not been expliictly condemned by the Church.[14]

3. *Those Who Are Under a Notorious Censure.*[15] This does not include those who are notoriously under a vindicative penalty, *e. g.*, under an *infamia iuris*,[16] although they might be excluded from gaining membership upon some other grounds. The natural law demands the avoidance of scandal and the removal of the danger of perversion which the admittance of such persons might entail. Or they might fall under the classification of public sinners.

[9] Cf. *supra*, pp. 47-48.

[10] Canon 693, § 1.

[11] Canon 1325, § 2.

[12] Canon 87. Relative to non-Catholics more will be said in the following article.

[13] Canon 2335.

[14] Canon 684.

[15] Canon 693, § 1. Cf. canon 2197, §§ 2 and 3; Chelodi, *Ius Poenale*, p. 4.

[16] Canon 2291, 4°.

4. *Public Sinners.* There is in the law no clear definition of a public sinner. However, the law points to certain elements which, when they are present, establish the necessary basis on which a person can be adjudged to be a public sinner. These elements are explained by the authors and supplementary indications are furnished by them whereby in an individual case it may be determined that the person in question is a public sinner.[17] A necessary element is the habitual and notorious living in the state of grave sin. As an example, one will consider as public sinners those who wilfully belong to condemned societies, those who are heretics, apostates, or schismatics, those who live in concubinage even though they were civilly married. Those who have failed to satisfy their Easter duty and those who are to be denied Christian burial are not expressly denied valid admittance into ecclesiastical societies unless they fall under the classification of public sinners. But in most such cases there would be present danger of scandal or perversion.[18]

The primary reason for not admitting any of the above mentioned persons into societies is the danger of scandal to others and of perversion to the members themselves. To this the Church has added a privative penalty [19] by law prohibiting the offenders from sharing the right of membership even when the danger of scandal or perversion is not present. However, if a candidate who falls under any of the above classes repents or is dispensed from the privative vindicative penalty, the prohibition ceases. Furthermore, since this prohibition applies to lay societies as analogous to approved societies, such a person could always be admitted validly to a lay society barring the danger of scandal and perversion. However, since it is

[17] Benedictus XIV, *De Synodo Dioecesana,* lib. VII, c. 11; Cappello, *Tractatus Canonico-Moralis de Sacramentis* (3. ed., Romae: Marietti, 1938), I, 74; Coronata, *De Locis et Temporibus Sacris* (Augustae Taurinorum: Marietti, 1922), pp. 264-267; Noldin, *Summa Theologiae Moralis* (25.-26. ed., 3 vols., Oeniponte-Lipsiae: Rauch, 1938-1939), III, 37; Augustine, *A Commentary,* IV (3. ed., 1925), 230 ff.

[18] Cf. Kerin, *The Privation of Christian Burial,* The Catholic University of America Canon Law Studies, n. 136 (Washington, D. C.: The Catholic University of America Press, 1941), pp. 160-232, in particular 225 ff.

[19] Privatio vel suspensio ad tempus pensionis quae ab Ecclesia vel ex bonis Ecclesiae solvitur, vel alius iuris seu privilegii ecclesiastici.—Canon 2291, 7°.

almost impossible to judge that such a danger will not be present, it is very improbable that such a one could be admitted except in the following case.

Article 2. Interdenominational or Mixed Societies

Perhaps the word "interdenominational" is misleading. It is employed to refer not only to a union of persons of different religious beliefs more or less on an equal basis, but also to a union of the faithful in which are admitted persons of other creeds. This latter circumstance does not change the nature of a parish society. It is still ruled by the faithful, and only otherwise would its status be diverse from that which attaches to parish societies. To it are admitted persons who are outside the fold of the Church of Christ, but who wish through it to attain the religious end of the society. Such persons, almost without exception, are in good faith in their religious belief. The former, strictly so called interdenominational societies, have no place among parish societies in the Church. But the latter, in which non-Catholics wish to associate themselves with Catholics for the achievement of the religious purpose for which the parish society exists, are not of necessity excluded. Hence they occasion a problem which demands some closer consideration.

A. *Parish Societies in Which Non-Catholics Are Admitted*

It was stated in the preceding article that non-Catholics cannot validly be admitted to membership in ecclesiastical associations. By analogy, this law was applied also to parish societies but only in so far as it was illicit to admit them. Obviously their admission is always valid. In certain instances it may also be licit if a distinction is made between non-Catholics in good faith and non-Catholics in bad faith. Those in bad faith must be barred from membership as danger of scandal and perversion would especially be present in admitting such persons. However, such danger need not always be present in admitting those who in good faith are separated from the Church.

The reason given by Schaefer for the prohibition of non-Catholics who are in good faith from joining associations in the Church flows from the forbidden *communicatio in sacris* and not from any consideration of indignity or unworthiness on the part of non-Catholics themselves.[20] Communication in divine services can take place in either of two ways, (a) participation by non-Catholics in Catholic services, and (b) participation by Catholics in non-Catholic services. There is no general law or prohibition against non-Catholics assisting at least passively in the divine services of Catholics.[21] On the other hand, the Code makes it licit for blessings to be imparted not only to Catechumens but also to other non-Catholics for the purpose of obtaining the light of faith or, together with it, the restoration of health, provided the imparting of such blessings is not otherwise prohibited.[22] Non-Catholics likewise are recommended to the benevolent attention of the pastors and the bishop.[23] Moreover it is hardly conceivable that their membership would always give rise to a forbidden participation in divine services. This could more easily or readily happen in confraternities, which are established especially for the increase of public worship,[24] but its likely occurrence would be rare even in pious unions, which are established for charitable and pious causes.[25] Far less rarely would it happen in a lay society, which has less frequent occasions of holding divine services than the approved societies.

The question of forbidden participation by Catholics in the services of non-Catholics is almost without point. If the society was predominately non-Catholic or governed by non-Catholics the occasion might arise. But if that supposition were the actual fact in a given case, then the society could of course no longer be classified as a parish society.

Furthermore, the Code forbids any kind of active participation or assistance in the services of non-Catholics.[26] Passive participa-

[20] Schaefer, *De Religiosis,* n. 623.

[21] This is not a question of the reception of the Sacraments by non-Catholics but merely of their assistance or presence during services. For specific prohibitions cf. canons 693, § 1, 1657, etc.

[22] Canon 1149.

[23] Canon 1350.

[24] Canon 707, § 2.

[25] Canon 707, § 1.

[26] Haud licitum est fidelibus quovis modo active assistere seu partem habere in sacris acatholicorum.—Canon 1258, § 1.

tion can be tolerated in certain instances,[27] but of this there is no question here. In a parish society which is governed and directed at least by the faithful, it is difficult to see just where non-Catholic services could find a place. If any non-Catholics did belong to a parish society, they would be members with the intention of fulfilling the end of a society which is attached to or connected with a Catholic church. The question would devolve into participation of non-Catholics in the services of Catholics as explained above.

Therefore it can be concluded that non-Catholics in good faith outside the fold of the Church can become members of parish societies provided there is no danger of scandal or perversion. It may, of course, not always be wise or advisable to permit them to join. Circumstances may persuade one against it. But if one can rightly abstract from all this, then the admission of such non-Catholic members may be tolerated.

The question of admitting non-Catholics could come up in any parish society except when the status of the society prohibit their admission into it. A society formed as a charitable society or an institution could very easily admit non-Catholics but such an institution would hardly be classified as a parish society. Another instance of such a society might be the Boy Scouts in the parish. Although the Boy Scouts are non-sectarian in themselves, nevertheless they require that each boy receive religious training according to his belief from his parents or from the church of which he is a member. A Boy Scout troop, then, established in a parish should have not only a temporal end but a spiritual one as well. Hence it could be classified as a parish society. It happens not infrequently that non-Catholic boys apply for admission in a Catholic troop. This has been permitted at times with great success. The same can be said of the Girl Scouts or any other organization of that kind. The admission of non-Catholic members can be permitted, but the activities of the entire troop should be under the direction of a priest.

[27] The Code permits mere passive or material presence at funerals, weddings, and other similar services when there is no danger of scandal or of perversion and a reasonable cause is at hand. In cases of doubt permission of the ordinary must be obtained. Cf. canon 1258, § 2.

B. *Strictly Interdenominational or Mixed Societies*

An example of a mixed or strictly interdenominational society is the so-called workingman's union. Although these unions are generally in no way religious societies, yet Pius X, in a letter to the German bishops, dissuaded Catholic workingmen from joining mixed societies.[28] However, if it became necessary for them to join such societies, the Holy Pontiff exhorted the bishops to employ special vigilance.[29] Pius XI committed it to the discretion of the bishops and ordinaries to permit workingmen to join neutral or mixed societies if Catholic associations could not be formed.[30] Necessary cautions were to be used to safeguard religious discipline and morals, especially by the erection of Catholic unions. Workingmen were not allowed to join non-Catholic unions unless there were formed side by side with them Catholic associations which would "have as their principal aim" the guarantee of full liberty of conscience to the Catholic members and "a thorough religious and moral training" and subjection to the mandates of the Church.[31] What are referred to here are rather the so-called religious brotherhoods, and not the strict labor unions. The Popes have often emphasized the right of the workingman to organize these unions, but cautioned against a religious element entering into them without ecclesiastical supervision.[32]

Article 3. Form of Reception

Among the various kinds of societies there seems to be but little difference in the requirements for valid admission to membership. In ecclesiastical societies formal reception consists in an authorita-

[28] Pius X, ep. encycl. *"Singulari quadam,"* 24 sept. 1912—*AAS*, IV (1912), 657-662.

[29] *Loc. cit.* "Regulariter reprobandas esse edixit Pius X . . . consociationes opificum mixtas, idest quae ex catholicis et acatholicis conflantur. Certis determinatis conditionibus tales societates mixtae autem tolerantur, sed Uniones Fidelium praeferendae sunt."—Schaefer, *De Religiosis*, n. 613.

[30] Pius XI, litt. encycl., *"Quadragesimo Anno,"* 15 maii 1931—*AAS*, XXIII (1931), 177-228.

[31] *Loc. cit.*, authorized translation—The Paulist Press, 1939.

[32] Leo XIII, *"Rerum Novarum,"*—*Loc. cit.*

tive act of receiving or of admitting the candidate into the society. This may be done by words or by some action signifying reception.[33] No special form is required. The law permits the statutes to regulate this.[34] Some more specific form is required, however, for admission into those societies which are erected as a moral person, for the Code demands the inscription of the candidate's name in the list of members for his valid admission into the society.[35] Membership in a corporation in civil law constitutes a contract between the members.[36] In other societies, lay as well as ecclesiastical, it constitutes at least an implied or a quasi-contract,[37] and consequently presupposes some agreement between the members to oblige themselves to the obligations of the society as expressed in the statutes and by-laws. This mutual exchange of compliance, or the agreement offered and received, constitutes the essence of admission into the society. Any method or form of reception is therefore optional as long as there is contained this mutual agreement.

Therefore mere internal consent does not suffice, for the essence of a contract demands more than an inward act. There would be no acceptance of the agreement on the part of the society itself. An agreement requires mutual consent. This requirement normally entails the non-admission of anyone who did not give any consent whatsoever, although there are exceptions to this, as in the sodalities of the Holy Infant, wherein the parents supply the consent of the infants.[38] Such supplied consent is furnished in the Sacrament of Baptism and certainly can also be given for a child's enrollment in a sodality. Prümmer contends that this can be done only in virtue of a special indult given to a particular society for the law in itself does not honor an admission as valid on the part of one who is unwilling or unknowing in the matter.[39] Infants, however, without

[33] *AAS,* IV (1868), 240, appendix V.

[34] Canons 692 and 694, § 1.

[35] Canon 694, § 2.

[36] Pomeroy, *Business Law,* p. 571.

[37] Vromant, *De Fidelium Associationibus,* pp. 35-36.

[38] *E. g.,* The Confraternity of the Blessed Virgin Mary of Mount Carmel. Cf. S. C. Indulg., *Cameracen.,* 29 aug. 1864—*Decr. Auth.,* n. 410; *Fontes,* n. 5071.

[39] Prümmer, *Manuale Iuris Canonici* (4. and 5. ed., Friburgi Brisgoviae: Herder & Co., 1927), p. 359. Cf. canon 693, § 3.

knowing or willing it, are capable of enjoying spiritual favors.[40] Lay societies for infants or young children were organized in the past, and many of them were commended and some even formally approved.[41] Therefore the consent on the part of the one who is capable by law of giving consent and also the consent of the society given and accepted on the part of both contitutes the essence of a member's admission. Whatever else is demanded for valid enrollment will be contained in the statutes.

Article 4. Rights and Duties of Members

A. *Rights of Members*

The rights of the members can be deduced from the manner in which they are mutually bound together in the society and from the statutes. If the society is a corporation or a moral person, then the rights of the members can be protected by law either ecclesiastical or civil. Since lay societies when constituted as moral persons no longer retain the nature of lay societies, they cannot enjoy the special rights granted to juridic persons in the Code.[42] But if they be incorporated in civil law, they do enjoy those rights which the civil law grants to corporations. Otherwise the members of societies which are not incorporated as moral personalities in Church law have simply such rights as are granted them in the statutes and bylaws. In regard to lay societies, which are not under the strict supervision of the Church, the combined rights of the total membership do not surpass the sum total of rights enjoyed by the divers individuals because the society does not exist as a new juridic entity. It can be said then that the rights of the society itself are as extensive as is the sum of the rights of all the members of the society.

A general principle which can be applied in connection with the right of the members of a society is the principle of law which is

[40] Vermeersch-Creusen, *Epitome Iuris Canonici* (3 vols., Mechliniae), I (6. ed., 1937), n. 791.

[41] Pius XI, motu propr. *"Romanorum Pontificum,"* 3 maii 1922—*AAS*, XIV (1922), 325; litt. encycl. *"Rerum Ecclesiae,"* 28 febr. 1926—*AAS*, XVIII (1926), 72; motu propr. *"Decessor noster,"* 24 iunii 1929—*AAS*, XXI (1929), 342-345.

[42] Canons 99-102; 1495, § 2; 1498; 1499, § 1; 1500; 1501; 1649.

contained in the Decretals: *Quod omnes tangit debet ab omnibus approbari.*[43] This principle is applied by the Code to ecclesiastical corporations,[44] but, being a principle, it applies to all societies alike. Therefore what touches or belongs to all touches or belongs to the individual. This flows from the nature of the union in a society, the members of which unite to attain some end through the sharing of rights and obligations. Nevertheless a principle admits of exceptions. If the statutes limit the rights of certain specified members, or of a certain classification of members, the principle is not thereby violated. But in the absence of any such authoritative restriction all the members enjoy the same rights and privileges.

Furthermore, all members validly enrolled according to the statutes, and not legitimately expelled or otherwise impeded, enjoy any and all the special privileges granted to a society. A special privilege can be granted by the competent authority within the scope of the law. For example, a lay society can be granted certain indulgences by him who has the power to do so.[45] Although indulgences are generally granted only to ecclesiastical associations, yet they can and sometimes are granted to lay societies.

B. *Duties of Members*

Rights and duties are correlative terms, *i. e.*, every right connotes a duty. The principle *quod omnes, uti singulos, tangit, ab omnibus probari debet* applies more to rights than to duties. However, rights cannot exist without duties. Although the law of the Church, especially the law governing societies, is much more lenient in granting rights than in imposing duties, nevertheless the prin-

[43] Reg. 29, R. J., in VI°.

[44] Quod autem omnes, uti singulos, tangit, ab omnibus probari debet.—Canon 101, § 1, 2°. The addition of the words *uti singulos* clarified the old law which was somewhat ambiguous.

[45] Vromant, *op. cit.*, p. 7. A bishop has by law the right to grant an indulgence of fifty days, and a cardinal of 200 days. Cf. canons 349, § 2, 2°, and 239, 24°. This power has been extended by a recent decree of the Sacred Penitentiary dated July 20, 1942. In this decree bishops were given the power to grant indulgences of 100 days, Archbishops of 200 days, and Cardinals of 300 days. Cf. *The Jurist*, III (1943), 157-158.

ciple mentioned above is applicable also to duties, even though it is applied more loosely and admits of more exceptions.

The observance of the duties imposed by membership in a society has always been strongly exhorted by the Church. She has always wished that the number of the faithful enrolled in associations be increased, yet not to such an extent that all be admitted indiscriminately. Especially should those be kept from joining who do not intend to fulfill the duties or gain the indulgences of the society.[46] Since indiscriminate reception to membership would only lead to a multiplication of societies in general and to the ineffectiveness of each society in particular, it would be better to bar from gaining membership those of whom it is known that they will not fulfill their duties. Still there is no strict moral obligation to observe the statutes, and therefore the lack of their observance is not a sin.[47] Yet the admission of those who do not intend to fulfill the duties would only tend to defeat the end for which the society was founded. There is indicated, then, the need to urge the faithful fulfillment of the duties and the observance of the statutes accepted freely by all who join.[48]

Since a society is formed for the purpose of attaining some specific end, those who take upon themselves membership in a society should accept the responsibility of aiding in the attainment of that end as expressed in the statutes. That is the main duty of each member. That responsibility grows out of the agreement or quasi-contract entered into by the member's reception into the society. Each member receives the right to enjoy the privileges of the society as a reward for the duties performed. That may not be the motive for anyone in particular when he joins a society. It may be less selfish than that which is implied in the expectation of a reward. A person may join simply to acquire a higher degree of sanctification.

[46] S. C. Indulg., *Urbis et Orbis,* 26 nov. 1880—*Decr. Auth.,* n. 453; *Fontes,* n. 5090. Cf. also S. C. Indulg., *Cameracen.,* 25 ian. 1842—*Decr. Auth.,* n. 298; *Fontes,* n. 5022; S. C. Indulg., *Constantien.,* 31 ian. 1848—*Decr. Auth.,* n. 347; *Fontes,* n. 5044; S. C. Indulg., *Massilien.,* 27 maii 1857—*Decr. Auth.,* n. 379; *Fontes,* n. 5058.

[47] Vromant, *op. cit.,* p. 34, n. 24.

[48] Wernz-Vidal, *Ius Canonicum,* II, 518.

Sanctification, then, is the reward of the duties to be performed. Or a person may join out of pure love of God or out of charity for the poor. Even though a reward is not expected, it is nevertheless part of the implied contract.

If a member fails in the performance of his duties it does not follow that he loses his privileges. For the enjoyment of these there is generally no other requirement than that of a valid enrollment.[49] This is true even in regard to the gaining of indulgences, except when special prayers or works are required.[50] Generally, in the past, a society was not allowed to make any special rules or to place in the statutes any special conditions for the enjoyment of these privileges.[51] However, the Holy See granted some exceptions whereby the faithful fulfillment of one's duties was made a necessary requisite for enjoying the privileges of the society. The most notable of these exceptions concerned the Society for the Propagation of the Faith and the *Pia Unio Cleri*. The privileges of the Society for the Propagation of the Faith could be enjoyed even without membership inscription as long as the conditions were fulfilled, while those of the *Pia Unio Cleri* demanded both the inscription of the member's name and the faithful performance of the duties.[52]

Strict lay societies do not fall under the present law. Inasmuch as they are private in character certain limitations of rights can be fixed in their statutes or by-laws to counteract all possible neglect of duty. When indulgences are made available for the membership certain restrictions can be placed upon the gaining of the indulgence by him who grants it. There is no limit to these restrictions. But,

[49] Canon 692; S. C. Indulg., *Massilien.*, 27 maii 1857—*Decr. Auth.*, n. 379; *Fontes*, n. 5058.

[50] S. C. Indulg., *Urbis et Orbis*, 26 nov. 1880—*Decr. Auth.*, n. 453; *Fontes*, n. 5090. Cf. also Vromant, *op. cit.*, p. 33, n. 24.

[51] Cf. S. C. Indulg., *Incerti loci in Gallia*, 12 febr. 1840—*Decr. Auth.*, n. 279; *Fontes*, n. 5014; S. C. Indulg., *Cameracen.*, 25 ian. 1842—*Decr. Auth.*, n. 298, ad 1 et 2; *Fontes*, n. 5022; S. C. Indulg., *Pinerolien.*, 12 maii 1843, ad 1—*Decr. Auth.*, n. 320; *Fontes*, n. 5030; S. C. Indulg., *Massilien.*, 27 maii 1857—*Decr. Auth.*, n. 379; *Fontes*, n. 5058; S. C. Indulg., 29 aug. 1864—*Decr. Auth.*, n. 407.

[52] S. C. de Prop. Fide, decr. 4 apr. 1926—*AAS*, XVIII (1926), 235-236.

even though the law of the Code does not specifically bind lay societies, it would seem that it should be followed, especially since it is in agreement with pre-Code law. The mind of the Church was to allow even negligent members the enjoyment of the privileges, probably because good will was shown by the very fact of enrollment in the society. However, the right to place restrictions still exists with the society, and such restrictions should be placed if negligence on the part of the members tends to impair the good which the society might do, or proves to be a detriment to the members themselves.

Article 5. Loss of Membership

A. *Renunciation of Membership*

In regard to an approved society renunciation of membership is more difficult than in a lay society. Since membership implies a quasi-contract, just as the consent both of the society and of the candidate is required for admission, so also the consent of both is required for the breaking of this contract, or for withdrawal from membership. Renunciation on the part of the member alone does not suffice.[53] Through membership certain rights and privileges are acquired. Privileges do not cease by renunciation alone, but by a renunciation which is accepted by the competent superior.[54] In civil law renunciation would or would not be sufficient depending upon the manner in which the society was united and depending also, if the society was incorporated, upon the State laws. But because lay societies have no special rights in the common law of the Church renunciation alone could suffice. Yet the implied or quasi-contract is still present. Hence such matters should be regulated by the statutes, which, in turn, should demand not only renunciation but also acceptance of this renunciation in order to safeguard the contract of membership.

[53] "Omnis res, per quascumque causas nascitur, per easdem dissolvitur." C. 1, X, *de regulis iuris*, V, 41. Cf. also Reiffenstuel, lib. I, tit. 35, nn. 112-114; Schaefer, *De Religiosis*, n. 640.

[54] Canon 72, § 1.

B. *Dismissal*

In the dismissal of members there are certain points common to both ecclesiastical and lay societies. No one legitimately belonging to an association should be dismissed except for a just cause according to the norm of the statutes.[55] The right which one acquires through his valid inscription on the rolls of a society cannot be denied any member, but a member can be dismissed by competent authority and for a just cause. The following points are necessary for valid dismissal:

(a) *Competent authority.* This authority is the same as the authority necessary to admit a member. He who can admit a member can also dismiss him. This holds good for all societies unless, for a special reason, a certain society give this power to a superior, *e. g.*, a priest.

(b) *Just cause.* The same reasons or causes that would prevent some one from becoming a member would also suffice for dismissal. If a member, then, fell away from the faith, joined a forbidden society, became subject to a notorious censure, or became a public sinner,[56] he could be dismissed. For lay societies, not only would these reasons suffice, with the restrictions, perhaps, discussed above,[57] but many other reasons not so strict would suffice, so that it can be said that any member can be dismissed simply at the will of the society. But there should be some reason for dismissal in virtue of the quasi-contract. Causes for dismissal are generally contained in the statutes. One such case could be, besides the above, the neglect of duty.

(c) *The form of dismissal.* Just as there must be a certain form of reception, so also there must be some form for dismissal. In ecclesiastical associations the manner of dismissal is required by law.[58] Three things are required: (1) a previous warning; (2) the society's

[55] Canon 696, § 1.

[56] Canon 696, § 2: Qui in casum inciderint, de quo in can. 693, § 1, expungantur, praemissa monitione, servatis propriis statutis et salvo iure recursus ad Ordinarium.

[57] Cf. *supra*, pp. 58-61.

[58] Canon 696, § 2.

observance of the form required by the statutes; and (3) the right of recourse to the ordinary. The statutes may demand two or more warnings, in which case one warning would not be sufficient for a valid dismissal. Likewise recourse need not have been employed in order that a member be actually dismissed but the right of having recourse to the ordinary must simply be open to him. However, in lay societies only the observance of the statutes is necessary. Neither a previous warning nor the right of recourse is required unless these rights be granted in the statutes.

CHAPTER VII

THE TEMPORAL GOODS OF A SOCIETY

Article 1. The Right to Possess Temporal Goods

The question of the administration of the temporal goods of a society presupposes that the society possesses goods in order to follow out its proper end. It scarcely seems possible for any association with a personal character to procure its end without goods, except that classification of societies known as *simple pious unions,* whose end is purely spiritual and whose members seek that end through works privately and individually performed, *e. g.*, the Apostolate of Prayer. Concerning associations erected as moral persons the right to possess goods is granted by the law itself.[1]

This is not true of an association merely approved or not possessing a written decree of erection. Much less is it true of lay societies. However, lay societies and merely approved societies, as well as formally erected associations, are societies in the strict sense of the word, for membership in them is effected by the free will of the faithful. All societies have from the natural law itself the right to possess goods,[2] as long as the end of such societies is honest and good in itself.[3]

If mere ecclesiastical approbation does not give a society juridic capacity for acquiring and possessing goods, it certainly does not take away the capacity which it had from the natural law antecedent to the approbation. For from the natural law a society which is organized for acquiring an honest end has the right (just as each individual man has the right to seek an end honest and proper to himself, independently from the concession of the positive law) of acquiring

[1] Canon 691, § 1. Cf. also canon 1495, § 2.

[2] Leo XIII, litt. encycl. *"Rerum Novarum,"* 15 maii 1891, n. 8—*Fontes,* n. 611; Pius XI, litt. encycl. *"Quadragesimo Anno,"* 15 maii 1931, n. 8—*AAS,* XXIII (1931), 186-189.

[3] Wernz-Vidal, *Ius Canonicum,* III, 514.

in a legitimate manner goods, money, etc., without which the end could not be attained. These goods, since they were either given to or acquired by the society, belong not to any individual member, but to the society itself to be used for its proper end.

In many cases there is no practical distinction between the formally erected and approved associations, except that the former acquire the juridic character of a person in the Church while the latter retain their own natural character. Both can be organized and governed in the same manner. But the former, besides their natural capacity, enjoy also through their authorized erection a juridic capacity by which their goods become, in a certain sense, ecclesiastical goods.[4] Through the approbation the Church recognizes a society together with its natural capacity. Therefore a society does not lose its natural capacity of acquiring and possessing goods through ecclesiastical approbation.

In this an approved society is similar to a society which is merely commended. Nevertheless it differs from the latter in that it is governed by the Church and is subject to the special laws of the Code to which a merely commended society is not subject.[5] Since, then, a commended society receives no special rights through its commendation by ecclesiastical authority, it receives no further right over and above its natural right of acquiring and possessing property or other goods.

Finally, a society which is not commended differs in no way from a commended society as far as rights and obligations are concerned in the common law. Neither is bound by the special laws on societies, but both are bound in the same manner as individuals are bound in the common law. Just as each individual man has a right to seek an end honest and proper to himself, so also not only approved societies but also lay societies have this same right as deriving from their natural capacity of acquiring and possessing goods as a means of attaining their end.

[4] Dominum bonorum, sub suprema auctoritate Sedis Apostolicae, ad eam pertinet moralem personam, quae eadem bona legitime acquisiverit.—Canon 1499, § 2.

[5] Wernz-Vidal, *loc. cit.*

Article 2. Sources of Income

A. *Initiation Fee and Dues*

One of the most common means of assuring a steady income in a society is the collection of dues. This is done for a twofold purpose: (1) to defray the expenses of the society, and (2) to furnish means of aiding the society in following out its end. Sometimes an admission or an initiation fee is charged. This is permissible, but the fee should not be so large that on account of it some are prevented from entering the society. The Code forbids the demanding of any entrance fee except that which is fixed and approved in the statutes.[6] This rule should be followed in any society. Both dues and initiation fee should be nominal. However, both should be regulated according to the necessity of the society in view of the end it proposes to achieve.

B. *The Collecting of Alms*

Besides the payment of dues, another steady source of income is the collecting of alms. It is called steady, and not stable, because such a means of income is entirely dependent upon the charity of the donor, which can be very unstable, even though a society depend continually or steadily upon it.

There has been much ecclesiastical legislation concerning the collecting of alms.[7] This has generally been in the form of prohibitions with reference to the collecting which was done without the consent of the ordinary. The present law also establishes a prohibition. It forbids the collecting of alms in general, but permits it under certain conditions. To this general rule the law establishes two exceptions in view of which a society is allowed to collect alms. The first ex-

[6] Occasione receptionis in associationem nihil directe vel indirecte exigatur, praeter id quod in statutis legitime approbatis designatum sit, aut ab Ordinario loci, ratione specialium circumstantiarum, expresse permissum in associationis favorem.—Canon 695.

[7] V Provincial Council of Milan (1579), Constitutionum pars III, n. XVIII—Mansi, XXXIV A, 483; Clement VIII, const. "Quaecumque," 7 dec. 1604, § 8—*Fontes*, n. 192; S. C. Indulg., *Cameracen.*, 11 iun. 1838—*Decr. Auth.*, n. 260; *Fontes*, n. 5007.

ception obtains when the statutes permit the collecting of alms. The second exception is verified when necessity makes such a demand provided, however, that permission has first been obtained from the ordinary.[8]

In ecclesiastical associations the statutes must be approved by the one who has the right to establish or approve the associations. If permission is granted therein to collect alms, it is equivalent to a general permission. Therefore it can be said that no society is allowed to collect alms without either a general permission, as contained in the statutes, or the particular permission of the ordinary, when he recognizes the necessity for it.

Other restrictions placed upon the collecting of alms concern the method in which the alms are collected and the persons who collect them. These restrictions are regulated either by the statutes, if permission for alms-gathering is contained in them, or by him who grants the special permission in particular cases.[9] Furthermore, if the alms are sought outside of the diocese in which the association is established, then the written permission of the ordinary in whose territory the alms are to be collected must be obtained.[10] Finally, the alms must always be used for the end for which they were given, that is, for the end for which the association was founded, unless they were given with a special end in view.[11] In all cases an account must be rendered to the ordinary.[12]

In view of both past and present legislation it seems that lay societies are not permitted to collect alms without the special permission of the ordinary. It is true that these societies are not bound by the special laws on ecclesiasical societies. Nor are they bound by past legislation, such as was enacted in the Constitution *"Quaecum-*

[8] Nulli associationi eleemosynas colligere licet, nisi id aut statuta permittant, aut necessitas postulet, et loci Ordinarii consensus accedat ac servetur forma ab oedem praescripta.—Canon 691, § 3.

[9] Canon 691, § 3.

[10] Ad eleemosynas extra territorium colligendas uniuscuiusque Ordinarii venia, scripto data, requiritur.—Canon 691, § 4.

[11] Canon 691, § 2.

[12] Oblationum quoque ac eleemosynarum fidelis erogationis rationem associatio reddat Ordinario loci.—Canon 691, § 5.

que," and which was either particular in nature or restricted to ecclesiastical associations. However, the Code forbids any private person, either cleric or lay, to collect alms or stipends for any pious or ecclesiastical institution, or for any pious or religious purpose, without the written permission of the Holy See or of his own ordinary and the ordinary of the place where the collection is to be made.[13] Hence, even though a lay society is a union of the faithful, nevertheless it is not official in character but merely private. A pastor is an official person just as is a bishop in his own diocese. Therefore he is allowed to collect alms within the limits of his parochial territory. But a lay society, not having been erected or approved by competent ecclesiastical authority, remains private in character. Therefore it is bound by the same law that binds private individuals. Like them a lay society may not solicit alms apart from a properly authorized permission.

However a distinction may be made with regard to the kind of collection that is solicited. In the strict sense a collection consists in the public soliciting of funds. In other words, the soliciting of money from relatives or acquaintances does not connote a real collection.[14] This would rather be a private petition and not a public collection, and therefore would not be forbidden. Likewise, if the contributions are made not out of charity but out of justice, such as payments for services rendered, then they are in no way to be considered as consequent upon alms-gathering. Again, if for services rendered no specified sum was stipulated, then the consequent offering is not to be considered as a form of donation, but rather as a form of wages. A case of this nature could readily occur in connection with a society of boys scouts in a parish. Such an organization may, for example, raise money by soliciting small jobs rather

[13] Canon 1503: Salvis praescriptis can. 621-624, vetantur privati tam clerici quam laici sine Sedis Apostolicae aut proprii Ordinarii et Ordinarii loci licentia, in scriptis data, stipem cogere pro quolibet pio aut ecclesiastico instituto vel fine. This is a repetition of the old law. Cf. C. 2, *de poenitentiis et remissionibus,* V, 9, in Clem.

[14] "Non tamen collectio eleemosynarum dicenda est privata petitio a non nullis coniunctis vel notis personis."—Vermeersch-Creusen, *Epitome Iuris Canonici,* I, 622.

than gift money. Out of these jobs small offerings may accrue. Even though the express purpose was that of raising money, and the solicitation embraced the entire parish so that it was in the fullest sense of the word a public solicitation, such a method of raising funds would not fall under the prohibition of the law, for in no sense can the payment for the services rendered be considered as alms, nor can the payment itself be considered a donation. Such a procedure would rather connote a licit and commendable way to raise funds.

C. *Donations*

Donations given to an association or to a society must be presumed to be given to help attain the end of the society, or at least to promote the benefit of the members. A donation made to a member of a society either in his capacity of an official, or at least in his status of a representative of the society, must be presumed to be given to the society. The person must be an official or a representative of the society. Otherwise the society itself or its end could not be the motive for the gift, and there could be no presumption in favor of the society. A presumption of law relieves him in whose favor the presumption rests from the burden of proof.[15] When a donation is made to the rector of a church it is presumed to be given to the church.[16] The same principle, by analogy, applies to societies. The presumption favors the society unless the contrary is evident or proved.

Donations to a society effect a transfer of ownership, so that the donating person loses the ownership which is acquired by the society. In no way can it be admitted that goods remain in the ownership of the one donating them until they are expended by the society to further its end[17] unless they were given and accepted with that under-

[15] Canons 1827 and 1747, 2°.

[16] Canon 1536, § 1.

[17] Wernz-Vidal, *Ius Canonicum,* III, 515; Cappello, *Summa Iuris Publici Ecclesiastici* (Romae: Marietti, 1923), n. 55; Vermeersch-Creusen, *Epitome,* I, n. 790; Ottaviani, *Institutiones Iuris Publici* (2. ed., 2 vols., E. Civitate Vaticana: Typis Polyglottis Vaticanis, 1936), nn. 123-125; Maroto holds the opposite view. But this seems to agree less with the mind of the society and of the donor as well as the common law.—Maroto, *Institutiones Iuris Canonici* (2 vols., Madrid, 1919), I, 550.

standing. Donations made to a church cannot be revoked.[18] This presupposes of course that the donation was given without conditional stipulations or reservations. In a conditional donation the conditions must always be fulfilled before the gift can become absolute. Otherwise complete ownership continues to vest in him from whom the society had hoped to receive the gift.

Since donations are given and goods are acquired only for the purpose of assisting the attainment of the end of the society, they must be used only for that purpose. This does not necessarily exclude the use of money for recreational purposes. For donations can be said to be given to a society not only because of the merits of the end of the society, but also because of the merits of the members themselves. Therefore it would not be an injustice to make use of the donations in such a manner, if that kind of procedure simply reflected a standing usuage or custom. However, the specifications of the donor must always be fulfilled. And, to ward off all possible abuses, the end of the society should always be foremost in the minds of the members.

D. *Other Methods*

There are other methods of acquiring property, but these have no further bearing upon ownership. Whether the property be real or personal does not matter as long as the title to it is legal. The Code even allows legal prescription as a means of acquiring a just title, provided that the attendant method conforms to the civil law.[19] However there are certain things which escape all hazard of alienation through the agency of legal prescription. These are plainly enumerated in the Code.[20] All requisites for an effective legal prescription are likewise listed.[21] Whether

[18] Canon 1536, § 4. The Decretals permitted the withdrawal of donations because of ingratitude on the part of the one who received them, but this law was not incorporated in the Code. Cf. c. 10, X, *de donationibus,* III, 24.

[19] Canon 1508: Praescriptionem, tanquam acquirendi et se liberandi modum, prout est in legislatione civili respectivae nationis, Ecclesia pro bonis ecclesiasticis recipit, salvo praescripto canonum qui sequuntur.

[20] Canon 1509.

[21] Canons 1510-1512.

property be acquired in this way or in any other way, ownership of it becomes established as long as the laws of the Code and the civil laws of the State are observed.

Article 3. Title of Ownership

The right to acquire and possess temporal goods presupposes juridic personality on the part of the one possessing it. Since, therefore, the right to form a society presupposes the right to acquire and possess all those things necessary to its existence and the attainment of its end,[22] it is easy to see why, under the canons, those who are minors, or those who lack juridic personality, have no right in the law to form societies. This statement of incapacity is not contrary to the statement that minors who have completed their fourteenth year of age can become members of purely spiritual societies, for the law itself gives minors of this age juridic personality in spiritual matters.[23] Similarly, since a lay society possesses no juridic personality inasmuch as its formation leaves it devoid of this characteristic, it cannot as such legally acquire and possess property or temporal goods. However, though the law grants it no rights in this regard, it does not follow that it cannot under some title other than a canonical title acquire and possess such goods. The omission of something from the positive statutes of the law does not at all necessarily imply an opposition between such an omission and that which is contained in the law. The moral law, the natural law, or the laws of justice, can give a just title beyond that of the positive church law. In other words, agreements, promises, and contracts, are morally binding even though they cannot be enforced legally. In a lay society the right to acquire and possess property is accorded by the natural law. The Code does not deny this right through the absence in its own law of any specific assertion or enforcement of the right in question. The legal title to the temporal goods of a lay society can therefore be invested in some member of that society who possesses the juridic capacity of ownership.

The same is true in regard to the civil law's attitude towards a

[22] De Meester, *Compendium*, n. 1439.

[23] Cf. *supra*, pp. 54-55.

society which is not civilly incorporated. The title to the property must be invested in some person, or persons (or be held by the society as a partnership, or in joint tenancy, etc.),[24] having juridic personality, otherwise the title could not be recognized by the law. For a society of minors property can be held in trust or under some other legal title. But if a lay society were incorporated in civil law it could hold property in its own name, even though its title of ownership would be without recognition in church law.

Article 4. The Administration of the Temporal Goods

A. *The Right to Choose an Administrator*

The right to acquire and possess property necessarily includes the right of administration. Otherwise there would be no true ownership. A lay society need not appoint a special administrator such as is mentioned for confraternities.[25] However, he who transacts business, disposes of property, or keeps the account of the expenditures, is in reality the administrator, whether he be appointed for a particular case or for a certain length of time. This appointment rests with the society. For the purpose of a society is the attainment of some end through a union of the faithful. Each one in the union or in the society has the right to strive for the attainment of that end. Hence each one has the right to voice his opinion, to vote, etc., unless these rights be restricted or denied by the statutes.[26] Therefore the right to appoint an administrator belongs to the society itself. If the statutes give this right to another, *e. g.*, the pastor, the members are simply exercising their right indirectly through another.

B. *Exemption from Ecclesiastical Supervision*

Since the right of the administration of its goods lies solely with the lay society, the administration itself, in so far as it does not in-

[24] Pomeroy, *Business Law*, pp. 50-52.

[25] Canon 697, § 1.

[26] This is based upon the rights of members as explained in Chapter VI. The principle of the Decretals is applied here: "Quod omnes tangit debet ab omnibus approbari."—Reg. 29, R. J., in VI°.

fringe upon any ecclesiastical rights, is exempt from any ecclesiastical supervision. A society has the right to acquire and possess goods. The acquisition of goods transfers their ownership to the society, as long as no conditional stipulation stands in the way of such acquisition. Such ownership includes the right to dispose of, invest, transfer, or administer the funds and the property according to the statutes. The statutes in turn do not have to be approved by ecclesiastical authority. Therefore the administration of the temporal goods of a lay society is entirely free from any ecclesiastical supervision.

In no way, then, can the money or goods of a lay society belong to a parish, even though the society was established by the pastor himself to aid in some parish activity. The goods remain in the ownership of the society, and the pastor has no more rights as a member than any other member. Therefore it would be unjust for some of the money to be appropriated for the benefit of the parish or the church without the consent of the society, unless the society was founded for that purpose. No matter how noble the cause, as, for example, some necessary repair of the church, the money cannot be used for it. Confraternities and pious unions officially erected by ecclesiastical authority retain dominion over their goods separate from that of the church to which they are attached,[27] even though these associations remain under ecclesiastical supervision. If their goods cannot be appropriated by the parish, certainly the goods of a lay society, which are not under ecclesiastical supervision, cannot be appropriated without the society's consent. The goods of a lay society remain fully under its own dominion. They remain in the ownership of a private group of individuals and must be disposed of according to their will within the limits of the statutes as long as the administration of these goods does not infringe upon the rights of others.

Being exempt from ecclesiastical supervision, lay societies are not bound by the obligation of rendering an account of their income. The obligation of rendering an annual report binds ecclesiastical associations.[28] But since the advent of the Code and the consequent

[27] Patrimonium confraternitatis et piae unionis, quae erecta sit in ecclesia non sua, aut cuius ecclesia sit simul ecclesia paroecialis, debet esse separatum a bonis fabricae vel communitatis.—Canon 717, § 2.

[28] Canon 691, § 5.

distinction between ecclesiastical and lay associations the latter are not bound by this law.

C. *How Income Must Be Used*

The use of the goods of a society depends upon the end or purpose of the society. Because the end is the motive for which the members unite, the first object in the mind of the members should be the attainment of that end. The society has the right to those things which are necessary to attain its end. If money or other property is necessary to attain the end, it can be acquired and possessed by the society. If, therefore, the money is expended for other purposes, then the society forfeits, in a sense, the right which it has by the natural law to possess goods. This does not mean that a group of people could not possess property for some other purpose. But a parish society founded for at least a partially religious end possesses goods in view of its right to attain that religious end. If the religious end failed totally, the society could still possess goods in order to attain a temporal end. But the society would no longer be religious in character and would fall from the classification of lay or parish societies. Its right to acquire and possess goods to attain a religious end would be forfeited because of the total disappearance of that religious end upon which the right was based.

There is also a question of justice in regard to the use of the money of a lay society. The administrator is bound in justice to use it within the limits granted him in the statutes or by the members. Alms collected or donations received must be used according to the will of the donor. However, if no stipulation or condition was made when the donation was executed, then the society becomes the sole owner. Use of the income for purposes other than the customary use [29] would not be an injustice, unless the funds were collected or received fraudulently, which in itself would create an injustice. Apart from this supposition the society, without violating justice, could use the funds for other purposes other than the customary ones. However, in view of what was said in the preceding paragraph, the closer a

[29] This includes expenditures for recreational purposes as explained above. Cf. *supra*, p. 76.

society adheres to the attainment of its end, the less danger there is of its losing its right to acquire goods. Furthermore, other than the customary uses can give rise to abuses which will alienate the society more and more from its religious end and gradually cause its corruption and dissolution.

From a legal standpoint the goods of a lay society are not ecclesiastical and therefore are not subject to the laws of alienation.[30] Since they are not ecclesiastical they are subject to the law of the land.

[30] Canon 1497, § 1; Vermeersch-Creusen, *Epitome,* I, 623; De Meester, *Compendium,* n. 1076.

CHAPTER VIII

ECCLESIASTICAL SUPERVISION

THE nature of a society is specified by its end. A society which has an essentially spiritual end is a spiritual society and, if it is not supreme in itself, is dependent upon the supreme ecclesiastical authority. A society which tends to promote some temporal good is a temporal society and its dependency is upon the civil power. However, an essentially religious end does not exclude secondary ends such as education, social activities, recreation, sports, and many other laudable endeavors.[1] Nor does it seem to exclude primary temporal ends as long as it does have a religious or spiritual end. Even if these secondary ends seem to predominate, in so far at least as the religious end is concerned, the society is dependent exclusively upon the ecclesiastical authority.[2]

If the temporal end and the spiritual end can be separated, then the Church and the State can claim jurisdiction over their own proper end. But if the two ends are inseparable, then the Church retains sole jurisdiction, for the spiritual end is superior to the temporal.[3] Therefore in every religious society the Church has the right of supervision. However, in lay societies not founded by ecclesiastical authority this supervision is restricted to certain points which will be discussed later. But in all societies it is exercised through the proper ecclesiastical superiors.

ARTICLE 1. MODERATOR AND CHAPLAIN

The moderator of an association directs the association, not necessarily as the president of the association, but according to the manner of a president in both its internal and external relations.[4] In this he is said to have true jurisdictional power according to the norms of the law and of the statutes.[5] He is charged with the safe-

[1] Cf. Bertola, *Il diritto ecclesiastico,* XLVIII (1937), 11.

[2] Ottaviana, *Institutiones,* I, nn. 109-111.

[3] *Ibid.,* nn. 82-84.

[4] Schaefer, *De Religiosis,* n. 627.

[5] Vromant, *De Fidelium Associationibus,* p. 52.

guarding of discipline. Hence it is his duty to care that the association increase both in number and spiritual fervor, especially by the careful observance of the statutes. He is also known as the *director* or the *rector*.[6] The Chaplain has charge of all sacred functions and ceremonies.[7] Though this office as such is distinct from that of the moderator, yet these two offices are not incompatible in relation to each other. The same priest can hold both offices.[8]

The offices of moderator and chaplain are proper to ecclesiastical associations. Relative to lay societies no specific provision regarding these offices is made. However, if there be a reasonable occasion for the existence of such offices in a lay society, which would almost always be the case at least with the moderator, provisions should correspondingly be made in the statutes of the various societies. This will enable the Church to bring such societies under her authoritative vigilance, and furthermore will keep them in closer harmony with the prescripts of the common law of the Church.[9]

A. *Appointment*

The one who has the right to erect or approve ecclesiastical associations has also the right to appoint the moderator and chaplain, unless this privilege is granted by an apostolic indult to the society itself, or to some other moral personality or physical individual.[10] If an indult is granted to the society the moderator and chaplain should be elected annually, unless the time is otherwise determined therein.[11] If the appointment is made by the ordinary, which is usually the case, then any priest can be named even though he is not the pastor.[12]

[6] Vromant, *loc. cit.*

[7] Schaefer, *loc. cit.*

[8] Canon 698, § 4.

[9] De Meester, *Compendium,* II, n. 1076.

[10] Canon 698, § 1.

[11] S. C. Indulg., *Corisopiten.*, 7 iun. 1842, ad 3—*Decr. Auth.*, n. 304; *Fontes,* n. 5025.

[12] S. C. Indulg., *Urbis et Orbis,* 8 ian. 1861—*Decr. Auth.,* n. 389; *Fontes,* n. 5062; S. C. Indulg., *Societatis Iesu,* 16 iul. 1887, ad 1—*Fontes,* n. 5103; S. C. Indulg., *Engolismen.,* 3 dec. 1892, ad 3—*Fontes,* n. 5116.

In lay societies the right of selecting the moderator and the chaplain remains with the society. If the moderator and the chaplain are elected to their offices by the society and are then presented to the ordinary for confirmation, the act of confirmation constitutes neither an approval nor a commendation of the society, nor does it confer upon the moderator or chaplain any special privileges. In no way does it give to them any of the privileges mentioned in the Code for moderators and chaplains. The confirmation simply implies that the priest presented is worthy of fulfilling the office. The duties of the office of moderator and chaplain are indicated below. However in lay societies additional duties may be indicated in the statutes.

B. *Rights and Duties*

Besides the duties mentioned above in the explanation of the offices of moderator and chaplain, the main duty of each consists in guiding or supervising the society. Since these officers are in close contact with the society, it is their duty to see that the society remains within the confines of the law. In this they have the right to supervise the activities of the society but their power over the members, *e. g.*, in correcting abuses and guarding the faith and morals of the members, does not exceed the power of the pastor and must be exercised under his supervision.

In ecclesiastical associations various rights are granted to the moderator and chaplain by the law. They receive from the law itself the faculty of blessing the habit, the insignia, or the scapular of the association.[13] Before the time of the Code this privilege was not granted merely by appointment, but by the delegation of special faculties.[14] Coronata holds that special faculties are still required.[15] But in view of the present law this does not seem to be necessary, at least not for the validity of the blessings. The offices of moderator and

[13] Canon 698, § 2.

[14] S. C. Indulg., *Caenomanen.*, 18 nov. 1843, ad 4—*Decr. Auth.*, n. 312; *Fontes*, n. 5029; S. C. Indulg., *Lemavicen.*, 22 aug. 1842, ad 2—*Decr. Auth.*, n. 306; *Fontes*, n. 5027; S. C. Indulg., *Lingonen.*, 30 ian. 1839, ad 1—*Decr. Auth.*, n. 270; *Fontes*, n. 5011.

[15] *Institutiones*, I, n. 683.

chaplain are true ecclesiastical offices in the strict sense.[16] Even though a priest may be appointed to such an office for a limited time only, nevertheless these offices are constituted by law, have stability, and confer upon the recipient at least some participation in ecclesiastical power. The faculty of blessing is attached to the office of moderator and chaplain. It is therefore ordinary power because it is attached to an office.[17] Because it is a power derived from the power of orders it cannot be delegated,[18] but it can always be used validly by him who holds the office [19]

The moderator has the right of receiving members into the society.[20] This right differs from the above mentioned power of blessing, for although it is a power annexed to an office, yet it is not derived from the power of orders but from the power of jurisdiction, and therefore can be delegated.[21] Finally, both the moderator and the chaplain, if they have occasion to preach, must follow the regulations of the Code on preaching.[22] This same holds true in regard to any sacred functions. The laws of the liturgy must be observed.[23]

Since the members of a lay society do not enjoy the right of having a proper habit of their own, a scapular, etc., the moderator and

[16] . . . stricto autem sensu est munus ordinatione sive divina sive ecclesiastica stabiliter constitutum, ad normam sacrorum canonum conferendum, aliquam saltem secumferens participationem ecclesiasticae potestatis sive ordinis sive iurisdictionis.—Canon 145, § 1.

[17] Canon 197, § 1. Cf. Vromant, *op. cit.*, p. 55.

[18] Canon 210. Cf. S. C. de Prop. Fide, decr., 4 apr. 1926, *Statuta generalia*, II, 12: Missionaries who are constrained to leave missionary countries because of sickness, old age, or obedience, retain the faculties of blessing the scapulars, etc., of the *Pia Unio Cleri pro Missionibus*. However this rule is not applied to all Pious Unions and it is not extended to include those missionaries who leave without any canonical reason.—*AAS*, XXVIII (1926), 233. Cf. also canon 1156.

[19] Canon 201, § 1. Cf. Beringer-Steinen, *Die Ablässe*, II, 95; De Meester, *Compendium*, n. 1079.

[20] De Meester, *op. cit.*, n. 506.

[21] Canon 199, § 1.

[22] Canons 1337-1342.

[23] Canon 2.

chaplain have no special faculties of blessing even if the society would adopt some special insignia. The habit of religious or of clerics cannot be worn by others unless that privilege be especially granted by law.[24] But nothing would forbid a lay society from adopting a special medal, *e. g.*, the miraculous medal, as part of the special insignia of the society. Even if the moderator or chaplain was approved by the bishop, such approval would not imply any special faculties. The moderator or chaplain has no more right than any other priest without faculties. Any priest can bless articles. But no priest can impart the proper blessing along with the specially attached indulgences to rosaries, scapulars, medals, etc., without special faculties. These faculties are reserved for those to whom the privilege was granted.

Article 2. Parish Supervision

A. *Rights and Duties of the Pastor Towards Societies in General*

The Code does not give the pastor any particular rights in regard to confraternities and pious unions or lay societies. Over the members of these societies the pastor has only such power as the Code gives him in virtue of his pastoral office. This office accords to the pastor the possession and the use of the ordinary power of jurisdiction.[25] But he cannot exercise this power except in the internal forum. The exercise of jurisdiction in the external forum implies the possession of legislative, judicial, and coercive powers. These are powers, then, which the pastor cannot exercise in virtue solely of his pastoral office. The pastor cannot make laws, pronounce judicial sentences, or punish transgressors with ecclesiastical penalties, for the exercise of these powers is reserved by the divine and the ecclesiastical law to the pope and to the bishops.[26] Only as a delegate of the pope or the bishops can a pastor function with authority in the external forum of the Church. As deriving from his office the pastor's jurisdiction is confined to the internal forum, except in the cases ex-

[24] Canon 683.

[25] Canon 197, § 1.

[26] Fanfani, *De Iure Parochorum*, n. 200.

pressly mentioned in law. When he exericises that jurisdiction he does so subordinately to his bishop and the pope.

The pastor is held *ex officio* and therefore *ex iustitia* to exercise the care of souls over all subjects residing within his parochial territory, as long as they are not freed of subjection to him either by the disposition of the law itself [27] or by the express will of the competent ecclesiastical authority.[28] His obligations in behalf of his parishioners are explained more fully by the Code. Omitting mention of those obligations which would rarely or never bear any relation to parish societies, one may here indicate that his duties include the celebration of the divine offices [29] and the administration of the sacraments as often as he is legitimately and reasonably asked for them by his parishioners.[30] He must know the sheep of his pastoral flock and prudently correct the erring, bestow his paternal charity upon the poor and the wretched, and use the greatest care in the Catholic instruction of youth.[31] He must, furthermore, diligently watch lest anything contrary to faith and morals be introduced in his parish, and he must also foster or institute works of charity, faith, and piety.[32]

Certain parochial functions are reserved to the pastor.[33] In regard to the sacraments he has the exclusive right apart from his local ordinary to administer solemn baptism,[34] to bring Holy Communion publicly to the sick, to carry Holy Viaticum either publicly

[27] Cf., *e. g.*, canons 514 and 1368.

[28] Canon 464, § 2.

[29] "Hic autem, sensu paulo latiori, eo nomine veniunt functiones omnigenae, quae sive in missali vel rituali continentur, sive in concilio particulari, synodo dioecesana vel ordinatione speciali ordinarii praescribuntur. . . ."—Beste, *Introductio in Codicem* (Collegeville, Minn.: St. John's Abbey Press, 1938), sub canone 467.

[30] Canon 467. Concerning the denial of the sacraments to the unworthy cf. canons 731, § 2 and 855.

[31] Canon 467.

[32] Canon 469.

[33] Canon 462.

[34] Canons 737, § 2; 738; 742; 759.

or privately to the dying,[35] and to administer the sacrament of Extreme Unction.[36]

Other reserved functions include the blessing of the baptismal font on Holy Saturday and Pentecost Saturday, the announcement of the proposed reception of Holy Orders by a parishioner in the near future, the proclamation of the banns of Matrimony, the assistance at marriage and the imparting of the nuptial blessing.[37] It is the pastor's right also to lead public processions outside of the church [38] and to impart blessings outside of the church with pomp and ceremony.[39] There are still other reservations by which the pastor is given additional rights just as there are other duties which he must perform. The ones here mentioned are sufficient, however, to explain what are the pastor's rights and duties towards the members of a parish society.

B. *Right and Duties of the Pastor Regarding Parish Societies*

The pastor's rights in regard to parish societies and the members of a parish society are deduced from the duties and privileges of his office. His duties regarding a parish society are the same as his duties in behalf of his parishioners. And if the members of the society belong to the parish, he is bound *ex iustitia* to fulfill these duties. Therefore, in addition to the administration of the sacraments, the pastor is held, in as far as the members are his subjects, to know them, to watch lest anything contrary to faith or morals

[35] Canons 847-849. Beste (*Introductio,* sub canone 847) holds that the repeated bringing of Holy Communion to the sick in the same danger of death is also reserved to the pastor. However this view does not seem to conform to the Code. He who is in danger of death is obliged to receive Holy Viaticum. Upon this obligation rests the pastor's right. If the sick person has fulfilled his obligation then the pastor has also exercised his right. Therefore any priest could again take Viaticum *devotionis causa* privately to the sick with at least the presumed permission of the priest to whom the care of the Blessed Sacrament is committed. Cf. canons 849, § 1; 864, §§ 1 and 3.

[36] Canons 848, § 2; 938, § 2; 939.

[37] Canons 998; 1022; 1094-1097; 1101.

[38] Canons 1290-1295.

[39] Augustine, *Commentary,* II, 537; Beste, *Introductio,* sub canone 462.

enter into the society, to correct and instruct the members, if necessary, and to encourage them in their works of charity, faith, and piety.[40] However, since he has no right to exercise jurisdiction in the external forum, he cannot make laws or punish transgressions with ecclesiastical penalties. He is not the *iudex in causis fidei,* but the watchman for the bishop.[41] Therein lies his power and his duty in supervising parish societies.

On the other hand, the duties of a society depend upon the rights of the pastor. Lay societies are independent of the pastor in both their internal and external government. However, they cannot infringe upon the rights of the pastor. The moderator or the chaplain cannot perform those functions which are reserved to the parochial office. The moderator or the chaplain cannot by reason of his office administer the sacraments of Baptism, of the Holy Eucharist, and of Extreme Unction, except in so far as their administration is permitted him by law.[42] Neither can he lead public processions or impart public blessings with pomp and ceremony without the pastor's consent. The members of a lay society are held to seek those things which are reserved to him by law or privilege from their own proper pastor. However, the members have the right to perform tasks of charity and piety, for such works are not reserved to the pastor, but simply committed to his care to institute or foster. It is the pastor's duty to institute such works if they do not already exist, to watch over them if they are already instituted, but not to interfere except in so far as he is allowed, for just reasons, to suppress lay societies.

[40] Parochus diligenter advigilet ne quid contra fidem ac mores in sua paroecia, praesertim in scholis publicis et privatis, tradatur, et opera caritatis, fidei ac pietatis foveat aut instituat.—Canon 469.

[41] Cf. Augustine, *op. cit.*, II, 555; S. C. S. Off., decr. 15 maii 1901—*Fontes,* n. 1254; Collectanea S. C. de Prop. Fide (1907), n. 2112; *ASS,* XXXIV (1900-1901), 383-384.

[42] Cf. *supra,* footnote 35. The moderator or chaplain, by reason of what has been said, can bring Holy Communion or even Viaticum to a sick member of a society with the permission of the pastor, or after the pastor has previously administered Holy Viaticum in the same danger of death, with at least the presumed permission of the priest to whom the care of the Blessed Sacrament has been committed.

C. *Supervision by the Parochial Assistant and Other Parochial Vicars*

The parochial assistant is a priest assigned by the proper ordinary to a pastor or to a parish in order to assist in the administration of the parish. His rights and obligations are determined by the diocesan statutes, the letter of the ordinary, or the commission of the pastor himself.[43] He is entirely subject to the pastor in all things that concern the administration of the parish.[44] But since he is assigned to the pastor because, owing to the size of the parish or for some other reason, in the judgment of the ordinary, the pastor alone is unable to provide for the complete care of the parish,[45] he supplements that care. Therefore, under the direction of the pastor, the assistant has the care of souls entrusted to him. He has only delegated power of jurisdiction, even though his work supplements that of the pastor in all things (except the application of the *Missa pro populo*).[46] However, he does have, besides delegated power, some kind of domestic power, the amplitude of which depends upon what is determined in his letter of appointment or by the pastor.[47] In his capacity of an assistant or helper of the pastor his rights and duties regarding parish societies are much the same as those of the pastor. The main point of supervision concerns the guarding of faith and morals and the fostering of charity and piety. Just as the pastor is the *watchman* for the bishop, so is the parochial assistant the *watchman* for the pastor.

Other Parochial vicars: Parochial vicars are priests who act in the place of the pastor or help him in the care of souls. To the latter class belong the parochial assistants. They are not *vicarii in iurisdic-*

[43] Canon 476, § 6.

[44] Canon 476, § 7. Cf. Fanfani, *De Iure Parochorum*, n. 454.

[45] Vermeersch-Creusen, *Epitome*, I, n. 569.

[46] Canon 476, § 6. Canon 451, § 2 seems to imply that the assistant has ordinary power. But the Code implicitly at least points to the power of the assistant as being of a delegated character by restricting it to the will of the ordinary or of the pastor (canon 476, § 6). This view is upheld by most authors. Cf. Fanfani, *De Iure Parochorum*, n. 473, B; Vermeersch-Creusen, *Epitome*, I, n. 571; De Meester, *Compendium*, n. 881, 1.

[47] Vermeersch-Creusen, *op. cit.*, I, n. 571.

tione, for the pastor cannot exercise jurisdiction in the external forum excepting when it is conceded expressly by the law. But they are *vicarii in divinis*, for they help the pastor in the administration of the sacraments and assume a part of the administration of the parish.[48] To the former class belong all other parochial vicars. Their rights and duties regarding parish societies will be briefly considered here.

(a) *Vicarius curatus seu actualis*. An *acting vicar* performs the functions of a pastor in a parish whose parochial title vests in a moral person, *e. g.*, in a parish which is incorporated with a religious order.. His rights and obligations are identical with those of a pastor.[49]

(b) *Vicarius oeconomus*. A *vicarius oeconomus* or an administrator is one who governs a parish during its vacancy. He has the same rights and duties as the pastor in the care of souls,[50] but is not allowed to do anything which will prejudice the rights of the succeeding pastor.[51] In general the *status quo* of the parish should be left intact, unless the care of souls demands otherwise. This rule would not, however, forbid the administrator to perform those acts which would better the condition of the parish.[52] Therefore it can be said that the state of societies should remain the same, unless evident necessity demands otherwise. However, the care of souls demands the same kind of watchfulness over matters of faith and morals at all times.

(c) *Vicarius substitutus*. The *vicarius substitutus* replaces the pastor during the latter's absence.[53] He holds the place of the pastor in all things that pertain to the care of souls, unless the local ordinary or the pastor has set some restrictions.[54] If therefore, no limitation

[48] Vermeersch-Creusen, *op. cit.*, I, 559.

[49] Canon 471.

[50] Canons 472-473.

[51] Canon 473, § 1.

[52] Cf. Fanfani, *De Iure Parochorum*, n. 433; Vermeersch-Creusen, *Epitome*, I, n. 563; Beste, *Introductio*, sub canone 473; Augustine, *Commentary*, II, 566; Prümmer, *Manuale*, p. 233.

[53] Absence considered here is either an absence of more than one week (canon 465, §§ 4 and 5) or an absence which results from a pastor's being deprived of his parish during the time of his appeal to Rome (canon 1923, § 2).

[54] Canon 474.

has been made, his power over societies is not restricted. However prudence dictates that the *status quo* of the parish remain intact unless the care of souls demands otherwise.

(d) *Vicarius adiutor*. A *vicarius adiutor* or a parochial adjutant is a priest assigned to a pastor who is suffering from some disability. His rights and duties depend upon his letter of appointment. If he supplies the pastor in all things pertaining to the care of souls his rights and duties are the same as those of a pastor (except the application of the *Missa pro populo*), but if he supplies only in part, then his power extends only to what has been granted him in his letter of appointment.[55] In the former case, therefore, he enjoys the same power over societies as any pastor, but in the latter case he enjoys only such power as has been expressly conceded to him.

Article 3. The Rights and Duties of the Dean

The *vicar forane* or the rural dean is a priest appointed by the bishop over a limited part of the diocese which embraces a number of parishes.[56] Besides the rights granted him in the diocesan synod or provincial council and the other rights conferred upon him by the Code,[57] he possesses the right of exercising vigilance over the deanery. He has no right to interfere with the administration of the parishes in his territory, but he must render to the bishop an annual report about the conditions existing in the various parishes.[58] The III Plenary Council of Baltimore (1884) advised the ordinaries to give their deans rather extensive faculties.[59] From the powers granted to a dean by the Code, his authority will be seen to consist more in the power to correct abuses in their districts than in the possession of any special power of jurisdiction. He cannot proceed in a judicial manner, for nowhere is the dean given jurisdiction in the external forum, but he can receive a denunciation or accusation, consign it to writing, and refer it to the local ordinary.[60]

[55] Canon 474. Cf. Fanfani, *op. cit.*, nn. 438-444.

[56] Canons 447 and 217.

[57] Canon 449.

[58] Canon 449.

[59] *Acta et Decreta*, n. 29, p. 19.

[60] Canon 1936.

Therefore the dean has the duty of watching over the faithful and the parishes in his district. If anything contrary to faith or morals or detrimental to the welfare of the Church arises or if any abuses crop up, he must endeavor to make the necessary corrections either by calling the abuses to the attention of the proper pastor, or by mentioning them in his report to the local ordinary on the condition of the parishes in his district. His authority over parish societies extends no further than his authority over the parishes in his district.

Article 4. Authority and Power of the Local Ordinary

The term *ordinary* is applied to one who holds an office to which the law itself has attached the power of jurisdiction.[61] It is applied especially to residential bishops and signifies their free and unhampered power in their own dioceses.[62] But it is applied to anyone who possesses full jurisdiction both in the external and in the internal forum, including the threefold powers, legislative, judicial, and coercive.[63] The term consequently excludes pastors, even though they do have ordinary power of jurisdiction. As has been seen pastors do not enjoy the free exercise of power in the external forum. Hence they are not ordinaries.

The Code expressly enumerates those who are included under this term.[64] It comprises "all who rule or govern a diocese or ecclesiastical district tantamount to a diocese"[65] as well as their vicars general, those who have the right of succession in the rule of such a territory, and certain religious superiors. The latter class of ordinaries however are not to be considered as local ordinaries.[66] All of the above have a potential jurisdiction over ecclesiastical societies.

As has been mentioned previously, ordinaries have no special authority over lay societies. Such societies, when they are not erected

[61] Canon 197.
[62] C. 1, X, *de officio iudicis ordinarii,* I, 31.
[63] Augustine, *Commentary,* II, 173.
[64] Canon 198.
[65] Augustine, *loc. cit.*
[66] Canon 198.

or approved by an ordinary, have no existence as juridical entities in the Church. Therefore he has no power over them in their nature of lay societies. However, since local ordinaries are the pastors of the souls of all who live in the diocese or territory committed to them,[67] they have the right and the duty of governing their dioceses in both spiritual and temporal affairs with true legislative, judicial, and coercive powers.[68] Therein lies the jurisdiction of the local ordinary. It embraces all of his subjects. Hence a lay society is under the jurisdiction of the local ordinary, not indeed as a society, but as a union which comprises his individual subjects.

A. *The Threefold Power of Jurisdiction*

1. *Legislative power:* Legislative power is the right of proposing in an obligatory manner those things which are necessary and useful for attaining the end of a society.[69] The right to make laws depends upon the necessity or usefulness of the means used to attain the end.[70] These means, in turn, are based upon the end of the society itself, and not upon any particular end cherished by a member or even a group of members. From this follows the obligation of all within the society to observe its laws, except those who are exempt [71] or those who are dispensed.[72] It is not necessary that the members of a society will first have chosen to accept the law before such a law can bind them as its subjects. Nor is there any right which

[67] Canon 334, § 1.

[68] Canon 335, § 1. Cf. Coronata, *Institutiones,* I, n. 394; Vermeersch-Creusen, *Epitome,* I, n. 405.

[69] Ottaviani, *Institutiones,* nn. 123-144. Cf. also Coronata, *Institutiones,* I, n. 15; Vermeersch-Creusen, *Epitome,* I, 450, 1; Van Hove, *Commentarium Lovaniense in Codicem Iuris Canonici,* Vol. I, Tom. II, *De Legibus Ecclesiasticis* (Mechliniae: H. Dessain, 1930), nn. 83-86; Cicognani, *Commentarium ad Librum I Codicis* (Romae: Ex Schola Typographica "Pio X," 1925), 519 ff.; Michiels, *Normae Generales Iuris Canonici* (2 vols., Lublin, Polonia: Universitas Catholica, 1929), I, pars. 1.

[70] Ottaviana, *op. cit.,* n. 24.

[71] Canons 618; 1491; 1492; etc. A clear example of this exemption is the exemption of non-Catholics from the juridical form which the law requires for the contraction of marriage. Cf. canon 1099.

[72] Canons 81-86; 291, § 2. Cf. Ojetti, *Commentarium,* I, 322-345.

allows the members an alternative choice in the matter of submission to the law.[73] However, a lay society is not a society in an ecclesiastical sense. No laws can be enacted by the local ordinary for a lay society except those which bind the whole community. The members therefore would be bound, not as members of that society, but as individuals in a community which is capable of receiving laws.[74]

The legislator, though he does not have the right of making laws in regard to individual members, can nevertheless issue precepts which bind individual members.[75] This right is based upon his legislative power of commanding or forbidding whatever aids or hinders the end of the society as a whole. In effect a precept is the same as a law, except in so far as it ceases with the authority or office of the one who gave it, and cannot be enforced in a judicial manner unless it was imposed in writing or in the presence of two witnesses.[76]

2. ***Judicial power:*** Judicial power is the right of declaring and proposing in an obligatory manner what actions conform or do not conform to the law and to set forth the legitimate effect of these actions.[77] The local ordinary has power over all ecclesiastical temporal matters as well as over all spiritual matters[78] within the limits of his own territory,[79] except in as far as these matters affect persons or things for whom or for which the law reserves judicial action to a higher authority.[80] Therefore within the limits of his competency the ordinary can personally or through his tribunal issue decrees or pass sentence upon the actions of his subjects. In the same manner he can exercise his power over the members of a lay society.

[73] Aichner, *Compendium Iuris Ecclesiasticae* (Brixinae, 1900), § 207, n. 3.

[74] C. 7, C. IX, q. 3. Cf. Ojetti, *Commentarium,* I, 75-79.

[75] "Praeceptum non necessario communitati legis recipiendae capaci, sed generatim singulis personis, sive physicis, sive moralibus datur."—Coronata, *op. cit.,* n. 31. Cf. Eichmann, *Lehrbuch des Kirchenrechts auf Grund des Codex Iuris Canonici* (2. ed., Paderborn: Schöningh, 1926), p. 33.

[76] Canon 24. Cf. Reiffenstuel, lib. I, tit. 2, nn. 43-45.

[77] Ottaviani, *op. cit.,* n. 26; Cavagnis, *Institutiones Iuris Publici Ecclesiastici* (4. ed., 3 vols., Romae, 1906), I, n. 105; Tarquini, *Iuris Ecclesiastici Publici Institutiones* (Romae, 1887), n. 20. For other writers cf. footnote n. 69.

[78] Canon 1553. Cf. Vermeersch-Creusen, *op. cit.,* n. 450, 2°.

[79] Canon 1572, § 1.

[80] Canons 1572, § 2; 1556-1557.

3. *Coercive power:* Coercive power is the right of using force upon subjects in order to enforce the law or in order to follow out the end of the society.[81] In ecclesiastical law this power is reserved to him to whom is given the right to make laws [82] but it can be exercised in relation to all those whom the legislator is capable of binding by law or by precept. This power is used when a penal sanction is attached to a law or precept, or also when the sanctioned penalty is inflicted for the violation of a law or a precept.

This threefold power of the ordinary must be used for promoting ecclesiastical discipline, for removing abuses, for safeguarding the purity of Catholic doctrine, and for preserving Christian morals.[83] This power can be exercised in relation to all his subjects. Hence, it includes lay societies, not in their nature of societies, but in their nature of constituting a group of subjects taken individually. Therefore an ordinary can issue precepts to a member or to all the members of a lay society. He can judge whether these precepts have been observed, or whether the laws of the community have been observed by the society, or rather, by the individual members forming the society. And he can punish all violations whether of law or of precept.

B. *General Vigilance of the Local Ordinary*

Although exempt from the authority of the local ordinary in both internal and external rule lay societies are nevertheless subject to his general vigilance. This vigilance is the same as the ordinary exercises over all his subjects. Primarily it extends over all matters of faith and morals.[84] It also extends to the laws of justice. Although matters of justice are included in morals, yet in the administration of property, income, etc., justice can be violated without any morally imputable guilt on the part of the society. The ordinary has a right in matters of justice to intervene, as also whenever the society infringes upon the rights of others.

[81] Ottaviani, *op. cit.*, n. 34. For other writers cf. *supra*, footnote n. 69.

[82] Cf. especially canons 2214, § 2, 2221 2223, and 2217.

[83] Vermeersch-Creusen, *op. cit.*, I, n. 451, 3.

[84] Canon 336, § 2. Cf. S. C. C. decr. 31 dec. 1909, c. XV, n. 144—*AAS*, II (1909), 33; S. C. C. decr. 4 nov. 1918, c. XI, n. 94—*AAS*, X (1918); 502; Vromant, *op. cit.*, p. 6.

C. *Special Vigilance of the Ordinary*

Besides this general vigilance the ordinary has the right of special vigilance when the society assumes the performance of a work, an obligation, or anything else which by law is committed to his special vigilance. This right of vigilance arises not from the fact that the society itself assumes the performance of such a work, but rather it arises from the nature of the work assumed. Again, the vigilance of the ordinary over the society is general, but his vigilance over the work is special in that it is committed to his special care by the law. This same vigilance would have to be employed over any other person assuming the performance of like works or obligations.

(a) *Collecting alms.* No one is allowed to collect alms without the consent either of the Holy See or of one's proper ordinary and also of the local ordinary of the place where the alms are to be collected.[85]

(b) *Devotions.* No new or novel devotions can be instituted, least of all those of a superstitious nature. Local ordinaries are charged with the duty of watchfulness over devotions both public and private, lest anything contrary to faith, strange to ecclesiastical traditions, or wearing the semblance of evil, creep into them.[86] Likewise notice must be taken of the law which forbids the reserving of special seats in a church without the consent of the ordinary. This consent may be given provided the rest of the faithful are not thereby inconvenienced.[87]

(c) *Mass stipends.* If any occasion should arise in which Mass stipends would come into the hands of a society, then the local ordinary will have the right to see that a record of them will be faithfully kept and that the obligations will be properly fulfilled.[88]

[85] Canon 1503. Cf. C. 2, *de poenitentiis et remissionibus,* V, 9, in Clem. Cf. also *supra,* pp. 72-75.

[86] Canons 336, § 2 and 1261.

[87] Canon 1263, § 2. S. R. C. *Entomilien.,* 11 dec. 1603, ad 3: "Posse Episcopum moderare arbitrio suo scamna et loca laicorum in Ecclesia, et providere ne unus solus multa loca occupet, ita ut pro aliis locus non relinquatur."—*Fontes,* n. 5207.

[88] Canon 842.

(d) *Last wills and testaments.* The local ordinary is the executor of all pious gifts, whether made by donation (*inter vivos*) or by last will and testament (*mortis causa*). This includes all movable and immovable goods left in trust, provided, of course, that they were left for a pious cause.[89]

(e) *Instruction of youth.* If any school, private or public, is founded by a private group of the faithful, then the local ordinary has the right of exercising special vigilance over the religious instruction of the children.[90] This, perhaps, will be a rare event. However, it may happen less rarely that a society will attempt to assume the task of giving religious instruction to children or to others who are in need of it. This kind of work must be undertaken under ecclesiastical supervision.

(f) *Other things committed to the special vigilance of the local ordinary.* Since other matters committed to the special vigilance of the local ordinary would less often be assumed by lay societies, they are merely indicated here. The most pertinent of these concern the celebration of Mass in private homes or domestic oratories,[91] private exposition of the Blessed Sacrament,[92] the care of relics [93] and the prohibition of books and the dissemination of literature.[94]

In general, the local ordinary has all the rights over societies that a pastor has. But while he is the *watchman* of his diocese he is also its superior. His jurisdiction gives him under the Holy See full authority over his subjects. He has authority, then, not only to watch, but also to command, to give precepts, to judge, to pass sentence, and finally to punish.

[89] Canons 1514 and 1515. Cf. Hannan, *The Canon Law of Wills,* The Catholic University of America Canon Law Studies, n. 86 (Washington, D. C.: The Catholic University of America Press, 1934), nn. 735-826, especially 775 ff.

[90] Canons 1381 and 1382.

[91] Canon 1194.

[92] Canon 1274.

[93] Canon 1279.

[94] Canons 1385, 1386, and 1397. Cf. also canons 1208, 1267, 1269, 1271, 1524, and 1544-1550.

Article 5. The Control of Parish Societies

A. *Relation Between Bishop and Pastor*

Before discussing the diocesan control of societies one may well recall briefly the status of the pastor in his parish, the status of the bishop in his diocese, and the relations between the two. The pastor exercises vigilance and pastoral care over all of his parishioners. He must show special benevolence, mercy, and charity towards the poor, the widows, the orphans, the ignorant, and the sick, bestowing special care upon them.[95] These are the special duties imposed upon him in virtue of his office.

The bishop, in addition to his other episcopal duties, has fundamentally the same duties in so far as the care of souls is concerned. But his office is performed through the pastor. While the pastor is, in a sense, only a watchman, the bishop can enforce discipline in a truly obligatory manner.[96] While the bishop is the pastor of all his subjects, he exercises this pastoral office through the pastors.[97] So long, then, as the pastor of a parish performs the duties of his office faithfully, the bishop should not interfere. And in this the Code protects pastors by demanding certain specified procedures for their removal.[98] This requirement of the Code does not prove that the bishop has no right unnecessarily to interfere with the work of the pastor, yet it strengthens and confirms the stability of the pastor. In this one sees an added argument in favor of what might be called the pastor's *subordinate autonomy.*

B. *Relation of the Society to the Parish*

The idea of a parochial entity in the Church has already been developed.[99] The idea is based upon the status of the parish on the

[95] Canon 467, § 1. Cf. Beste, *Introductio,* sub canon 467.

[96] Cf. preceding Article.

[97] Even though the bishop exercises his pastoral office through the pastors, yet he is truly the direct and immediate pastor of all souls, because he has the power and the right to appoint pastors. Cf. canon 455. Furthermore he is charged to perform some pastoral duties himself, *e.g.,* preaching. Cf. canon 1327.

[98] Canons 2147-2175 and 2182-2185.

[99] Cf. *supra,* p. 33.

one hand, and the rights and obligations of the pastor on the other. However, it will not be superfluous to repeat that the pastor has the duty of ministering to all who live within the parochial limits. The faithful, in turn, have the right to this ministry. The right of one is based upon the duty of the other. When, therefore, a certain group of the parishioners unites or forms a parish society, it takes upon itself certain tasks, whether of piety, of charity, or of personal sanctification, which the law commits to the pastors to institute or to foster.[100] Ordinarily this endeavor of the faithful does not infringe upon the rights of the pastor. Rather under his counsel and guidance such a union constitutes an aid in his parochial duties. With the prudent guidance of the pastor and the good will of the members of the society, every parish society can and should contribute to the general good of the parish by means of its specialized activity.

C. *Diocesan Control*

In speaking of the decline of the social order Pius XI deplored the prevalent trend to centralized control. This trend tends to render extinct associations which formerly carried some of the burden of the State. The following is an excerpt applicable to the point in question:

> It is indeed true, as history clearly proves, that owing to the change in social conditions, much that was formerly done by small bodies can nowadays be accomplished only by large corporations. None the less, just as it is wrong to withdraw from the individual and commit to the community at large what private enterprise and industry can accomplish, so, too, it is an injustice, a grave evil and a disturbance of right order for a larger and higher organization to arrogate to itself functions which can be performed efficiently by smaller and lower bodies. This is a fundamental principle of social philosophy, unshaken and unchangeable, and it retains its full truth today. Of its very nature the true aim of all social activity should be to help individual members of the social body, but never to destroy or absorb them.[101]

[100] Canon 469.

[101] Litt. encycl. "*Quadragesimo Anno,*" 15 maii 1931—*AAS,* XXIII (1931), 188-189. Authorized translation by The Paulist Press (New York, 1939).

It is true that Pius XI was referring to civil society in his encyclical letter. The above mentioned excerpt is not applicable in its entirety to parish societies without some restrictions. For example, it is not always an injustice if the pastor or ordinary refuses to permit their formation or orders their suppression.[102] But the basic principle underlying the statement of Pius XI is nevertheless applicable to parish societies.

The parish is a social unit. If within it there form other social units, which can be of assistance in attaining the end of the parochial social unit, these units should be allowed to exist. It would, then, be against good social order for a diocese to assume exclusive control of parish societies, for such an act would constitute an infringement upon the natural rights of these societies. It would likewise be against good social order for a parish to assume all the tasks which could be performed by societies. Good social order dictates that smaller parochial social units be permitted to assume tasks, perform works of charity and piety, etc., if these units can fulfill them efficiently and do not constitute a danger of infringing upon the rights of the pastor.[103]

Diocesan control of societies does not necessarily underlie diocesan or centralized units of societies. By these are meant diocesan unions of societies through which individual parish units operate, such as have been established for the Catholic Youth Organization, the Catholic Charities, etc.[104] These units should serve as aids to the parish societies and in no way should rule or govern them. Likewise diocesan control of societies does not necessarily underlie extant diocesan societies. These latter can be founded to attain some end which does not fall under the vigilance of the pastor or which is not

[102] Cf. *infra*, pp. 118-122.

[103] For a detailed discussion of the rights of the pastor cf. *supra*, pp. 121-122. The principal pastoral rights which a society might violate would be the rights which the pastor has in the exercise of charity towards the poor and the sick. Cf. canon 469.

[104] Although organizations of this nature are often erected by the local ordinary, and therefore are ecclesiastical in character, yet the individual parish units remain lay societies, unless they have been canonically erected or at least authoritatively approved. Cf. *supra*, pp. 35-36.

specially reserved to the vigilance of the ordinary.[105] But if any society, union of societies, or diocesan organization, "arrogates to itself functions which can be performed efficiently by smaller and lower bodies," or infringes upon the rights of the pastor, such an action constitutes, if not an injustice, at least a disturbance of right order.

[105] Cf. *supra*, pp. 97-98.

CHAPTER IX

REDRESS AGAINST WRONGS

ARTICLE 1. THE ECCLESIASTICAL TRIBUNAL

SINCE lay societies are not ecclesiastical moral persons they have as such no juridic rights. They are not even considered as minors, and hence cannot be represented in law by their president or other officer. To an ecclesiastical tribunal a lay society is simply a number of individuals possessing juridic personality in as far as the law recognizes each one individually as possessing it.

In an ecclesiastical society erected as a moral person, special or corporate rights are enjoyed. If, for example, anyone applies the money of an association to himself or distributes it among others, he sins against justice. He violates justice not against the members but against the society itself.[1] The society itself can institute a legal action to recover the money.

If, however, some one appropriates the money of a lay society, he likewise violates justice against the society, and according to the moral or natural law must restore it to the society. But according to the Canon Law he does not violate the rights of the society which in law possesses no juridic personality. He does, however, violate the rights of him who in law enjoyed juridic personality and was capable of ownership, *e.g.*, as trustee for the society. Hence a suit could not be entered either by the society or against the society, but only by or against individuals.

From what has been said it must not be concluded that lay societies have no means of obtaining legal protection in the ecclesiastical tribunal as well as in the civil courts. Canon Law provides various kinds of suits, especially in civil or contentious cases whereby a plaintiff may vindicate his rights.[2] These various kinds of suits re-

[1] Wernz-Vidal, *Ius Canonicum,* III, 515.

[2] Canons 1667-1705.

spond quite completely to the need for anyone to vindicate his rights, hence no mention need be made of them here. A pertinent distinction is found in the civil law distinction of real, mixed, and personal actions at court. Real actions at court answer the purpose of recovering real property. Mixed actions at court answer the purpose of recovering real property and the damages for the injury inflicted upon it. Personal actions at court answer the purpose of recovering money or personal property.[3] Although the Code does not use this threefold distinction it provides actions correspondingly.

Therefore the means which a lay society possesses to redress wrongs committed against them, are the same as any individual possesses. The society cannot sue in its own name. It cannot juridically designate a representative from the society to sue in its name. But any member capable by law of bringing suit[4] may institute such an action before the ecclesiastical court, which will uphold the laws of justice and of morals as well as ecclesiastical laws.

Article 2. The Civil Tribunal

A. *Incorporated Societies*

The status of an unincorporated society in civil law is comparable to that of a lay society in Canon Law. However, a lay society can be incorporated in civil law, even though it can never as such exist as an ecclesiastical moral person, for by ecclesiastical erection it would cease to be a lay society.[5] A civil corporation is an "organization of persons endowed by law to act, within certain limits, as a natural person."[6] It is known as "a perpetual succession of individuals . . . capable of acting for the promotion of a particular object, like one immortal being."[7] It is created only by the express or implied authority of the government. This authority resides with

[3] Pomeroy, *op. cit.*, p. 28.

[4] Relative to those whom the law renders incapable cf. canons 1648, § 1, 1649, 1650, and 1652.

[5] Cf. *supra*, pp. 30-31.

[6] Pomeroy, *Business Law*, p. 547.

[7] Dartmouth College v. Woodward, 4 Wheat (U. S.), 518.

the various states. But in general, upon application, a charter of incorporation is issued, under a special or general act of assembly, in which is contained mention of the rights and obligations of the corporation.[8]

The legal effects on incorporation are exemplified principally in the corporate rights of the members. The society itself has the right to resort to legal action and, in turn, legal action can be resorted to against it. It possesses juridic personality and thus can be a plaintiff or a defendant. "It holds property, is sued and sues in its own name, and, in general, is solely liable for its obligations."[9] Probably its most important characteristic is the fact that the body continues to exist irrespective of its membership. Loss of members or the addition of new members does not change the rights and obligations. Thus legal action can be instituted against a corporation even though the members who perpetrated an injustice no longer belong to it.

B. *Unincorporated Societies*

From the rights of civilly incorporated society can be deduced the status of an unincorporated society. As in Canon Law, such a society has no legal status. It is not recognized as a moral entity. Hence any legal action would have to be instituted not against the society, but against the individual member or members. Likewise the society itself cannot enter a legal suit. Only the individual members who have legal capacity can institute a legal action. From this it follows that only an incorporated society can be protected as a society in civil law. In addition to the benefit of this protection an incorporated society would receive the benefit of continued legal existence irrespective of its members. Furthermore, it would acquire no legal entanglements as it need never use the charter. Nevertheless, these benefits would rarely prove of sufficient value to warrant incorporation in civil law as a lay society is a private group using private funds to attain some religious end. In view of its end civil incorporation would rarely be beneficial or necessary.

[8] Pomeroy, *op. cit.*, p. 555.

[9] *Ibid.*, p. 547.

C. *The Privilege of the Forum*

The privilege of the forum is a privilege enjoyed by specified persons whereby they are exempt from the jurisdiction of the civil courts. This exemption is not absolute. It can, in most cases, be suspended by the permission of the competent superior. All clerics enjoy the privilege of the forum.[10] They cannot be brought before the civil courts without the permission of the local ordinary.[11] Likewise all men and women religious[12] and novices,[13] and also the members and novices of a community who lead a life in common after the fashion of the religious life, but who are not professed with religious vows,[14] enjoy this privilege. To institute legal action against them in the civil courts requires, as with clerics, the permission of the local ordinary.

This privilege of the forum may be applicable to lay societies in as far as the pastor, the assistant, some other priest, or even a cleric, was connected with the administration of the goods of the society. If an injustice was committed, even though inadvertently, suit could always be entered against the cleric before the ecclesiastical tribunal. However, such a suit could not be instituted before the civil courts without the permission of the proper ecclesiastical superior, that is, the local ordinary.

Article 3. Penalties Applicable to Lay Societies

The discussion of the number and kinds of ecclesiastical penalties has no connection with the study of lay societies. A lay society cannot incur a penalty. The members of a lay society can incur a penalty only in so far as any other person can incur one. But because the members of a lay society assume of their own free will the attainment of some religious end, it is more easily possible that the members will infringe upon ecclesiastical rights precisely in view of the fact that such members, unlike others, carry on a work

[10] Canon 120.

[11] Canon 120, § 2.

[12] Canon 488, 7°.

[13] Canon 614.

[14] Canon 680.

in which the possibility of a clash or conflict is ever present. Hence the penalties attached to certain violations of the law or to the infringement upon the rights of the Church may be mentioned here.

1. *Crimes against religion.* These crimes on the part of lay persons consist mainly of blasphemy, of perjury out of court, of superstitious practices, of the perpetration of sacrilege, of the fabrication of false relics, of their sale, distribution and exposure for public veneration when they are known to be spurious, of the seeking of financial gain through traffic in indulgences, of the violation of corpses or tombs for some evil end, and of the violation of churches and of cemeteries.[15]

2. *Crimes against Ecclesiastical Authority.* Pertinacious disobedience to ecclesiastical authority, recourse to the lay power for the sake of setting up obstacles to the promulgation or execution of acts and decrees emanating from the Holy See, the enactment of legal instruments militating against the rights and liberties of the Church, and the hindering of the Church in the exercise of her jurisdiction through the intervention of lay power are crimes for which the Church has enacted penalties.[16] Likewise the depriving of a cleric of the privilege of the forum, *i. e.*, the citing of a cleric before the civil court without the local ordinary's permission, is punishable by law.[17] Finally, injuries against the hierarchy whether verbal or real,[18] the usurpation of ecclesiastical property, movable or immovable,[19] and the failure to fulfill last wills and donations made for pious causes,[20] are also punishable by law.

3. *Crimes against good name, property, liberty, or life.* These crimes are of a general character and can be punished in various ways. As in all crimes against justice, restitution is demanded, but other penalties as well can be inflicted.[21]

[15] Canons 2320-2329. Cf. Blat, *Commentarium Textus Codicis Iuris Canonici* (6 vols., Romae: Collegio "Angelico," 1921-1927), VI (*De Delictis et Poenis*), 207-218.

[16] Canons 2331-2334.

[17] Canon 2341.

[18] Canons 2344 and 2345.

[19] Canon 2346.

[20] Canon 2348.

[21] Canons 2354-2355. Cf. Blat, *op. cit.*, pp. 246-265.

4. *Crimen Falsi.* This classification of crimes refers to the falsification of papal letters, decrees, or rescripts and the punishment embraces both those who forge or falsify documents and those who knowingly use them.[22] Those who fraudently or deceitfully suppress the truth or state a falsehood in a petition for a rescript addressed to the Apostolic See or to the local ordinary may be punished by the latter according to the grievousness of their guilt.[23] Those who forge or falsify other ecclesiastical letters or acts, public or private, as well as those who knowingly make use of such spurious documents are liable to the same punishment.[24]

Every crime, which is an external and morally imputable violation of the law, presupposes grave guilt on the part of the delinquent.[25] Hence, to know whether or not a penalty is incurred is an entirely different question than to know which crimes are punishable by law or which crimes have penalties attached to them, whether specific or at least indeterminate.[26] For the purpose of the present study it is enough to know which crimes stand punishable in the law and which crimes may be perpetrated by the members of a lay society in view of the special work which they assume.

Article 4. Recourse and Appeal

A. *Definition and Notion*

"Recourse is the act of referring to a higher authority the administrative decision, precept or decree of some superior." [27] An appeal, in the technical sense of the term is "an act by which a party to a trial invokes the aid of a superior judge against the judicial decree or sentence of an inferior judge." [28] A recourse and an ap-

[22] Canon 2360.

[23] Canon 2361.

[24] Canon 2362.

[25] Canon 2195, § 2.

[26] Canon 2195, § 1. For a further study of penalties cf. Roberti, *De Delictis et Poenis* (Romae: Apud Aedes Facultates Iuridicae ad Apollinaris, 1938), especially nn. 70-150; Augustine, *Commentary*, Vol. VIII, 9-57. Blat, *op. cit.*; Michiels, *De Delictis et Poenis* (Lublin: Universitas Catholica, 1934), 138 ff.

[27] Lydon, *Ready Answers in Canon Law* (New York-Cincinnati-Chicago-St. Louis-San Francisco: Benziger Brothers, 1934), under *recourse*.

[28] *Ibid.*, under *appeals*.

peal are in their ultimate effect similar. They differ only in that recourse is granted in administrative procedures while appeal is granted in judicial procedures. Their purpose is to seek redress against alleged injustice or error, or at least to make sure that justice has been properly administered. The natural law of justice does not demand that appeals be allowed, but it does demand that some legal remedy be open to one who has been injured.[29] The Code, unless it expressly forbids it, leaves the way open for recourse and appeal. The immediate result of an interposed recourse or appeal is that the decree or sentence is either suspended or not suspended in its execution. The normal result of a recourse is that the decree is not suspended,[30] but in an appeal there is normally implied a suspended sentence.[31] In line with these general norms the decree against which recourse is sought remains in force and therefore must be obeyed while the recourse is pending. But in an appeal the execution of the sentence is stayed until the higher court reaffirms the sentence. As long as the sentence of the lower is not reaffirmed, the verdict of that court is without judicial effect.[32]

By way of departure from these general norms there are cases in which recourse does suspend the execution of the decree,[33] just as there are cases in which an appeal does not suspend the execution of the judicial sentence.[34]

Since only formal judicial sentences can be appealed, this form of redress is not pertinent here. Lay societies are not juridic persons and therefore, as such, could not be subject to judicial action. Therefore recourse alone will be considered in regard to lay societies.

B. *Recourse Against Dismissal and Suppression*

1. *Ecclesiastical Societies.* The Code grants to members of ecclesiastical societies the right of recourse in cases of dismissal from

[29] *Ibid.*, under *appeals*.

[30] Cf. canons 106, 6°; 296, § 2; 298; 345; 454, § 5; 513, § 2; 1340, § 3; 1395, § 2; 1428, § 3; 2243, § 1.

[31] Canon 1889, § 2. A provisional execution of a sentence is provided for by canon 1917.

[32] Canon 1889, § 1.

[33] Canons 647, § 2, 4°; 2243, § 2; 2287.

[34] Canons 2243, § 1; 1880.

the association.[35] There is some dispute concerning the immediate result of such a recourse, but in line with the general principles on recourse, and in agreement with most of the authors,[36] the recourse does not suspend the decree of dismissal from its execution. On the other hand, there is likewise a disagreement concerning the immediate result of a recourse interposed by a society against a decree of suppression. In line again with the general rule such a recourse should be considered as not having a suspensive effect upon the decree of suppression.[37] However there are some adherents of the opposite view who contend that such a recourse does have a suspensive effect.[38]

It seems necessary to advert to the distinction between a *penal* decree of suppression and a *contentious* decree of suppression.[39] If the suppression be *contentious* in character, then according to the normal rule the recourse against it will not be one with a suspensive effect. If the suppression be *penal* in character, then the penalty is of the nature of a vindicative penalty.[40] Against an inflicted vindicative penalty the law in Canon 2287 states that a recourse as well as an appeal is recognized as having a suspensive effect as long as no contrary specific provision is made. No such provision appears anywhere in the law regarding recourse against a penal decree of suppression. Hence it seems that the interposition of a recourse against such a decree will stay its execution until the authority with whom the recourse rests has reaffirmed the original decree.

[35] Canon 696, § 2.

[36] Cf. Vromant, *De Fidelium Associationibus*, p. 49; Schaefer, *De Religiosis*, n. 625; Blat, *Commentarius Textus Codicis Iuris Canonici*, II, 669; Reiffenstuel, lib. II, tit. 29, n. 11.

[37] Vromant, *op. cit.*, p. 58; Goyeneche, *Iuris Canonici Summa Principia, Partes II (De Religiosis) et III (De Laicis) Libri II Codicis* (Romae: Tip. Pol. "Cuone di Maria," 1938), p. 258, footnote 37.

[38] Cf. Blat, *op. cit.*, II, 669; Schaefer, *De Religiosis*, n. 628, 2; Cocchi, *Commentarium in Codicem Iuris Canonici* (8 vols., Taurini, 1925-1930), IV, 182, 1.

[39] *Contentious* is used here in contradistinction to penal and connotes a controversy and not a crime. Cf. canon 1552, § 2, 1°. In this sense it does not necessarily imply judicial processes but rather administrative processes.

[40] Canon 2291, 3°. Suppression of societies is not listed as a vindicative penalty but suppression of a parish, etc. Suppression always partakes of the nature of a vindicative penalty if it is in the nature of a penalty. The other vindicative penalties mentioned in canon 2291 can also be applicable to lay societies.

It seems likewise necessary to draw attention to the distinction that exists between a *decree of suppression* and the *penal threat of suppression.* If there is question only of the *penal threat of suppression,* then it appears necessary to assume that the law will fortify the recourse against the threatened penalty with a suspensive effect, especially since the law grants this same legal force to a recourse even when it is interposed against the penal decree of suppression. And if the recourse be of suspensive effect when it is concerned with the penalty as such, then *a fortiori,* according to the analogy of Canon 2243, § 2, the recourse will have the same suspensive effect when it is concerned with the precept which inheres in the penal threat of suppression.

Hence the law of Canon 2287 seems to apply whenever there is question of the penal suppression of a society, whether the recourse be undertaken (1) against the penal decree of suppression; (2) the penal threat of suppression, or (3) the precept inherent in that threat.

The application of these principles to societies is evident depending upon the reasons for which the society is suppressed. A society can be suppressed either because (a) it fails to do sufficient good or conflicts with a society of the same nature, or (b) it is the cause of scandal or its members are guilty of some act partaking of the nature of a crime.[41] In the first case recourse against suppression would not have a suspensive effect because the society is suppressed only for contentious or controversial reasons, *e.g.,* the ordinary, or the pastor, either of whom are competent in such a case, decides that the poor or the sick can be better cared for by some other means. If, therefore, he orders the society disbanded, it has the right of recourse, but while the recourse is pending the society cannot function.[42]

In the second case, however, suppression can be considered in the nature of a penalty. Suppression of a society is not included in the list of vindicative penalties mentioned in the Code,[43] but this list

[41] Cf. *infra,* p. 118.

[42] The pastor's rights in suppressing a society are limited. This is discussed in the following chapter.

[43] Canons 2291-2297.

is not all-inclusive. The fact that the Code lists as a vindicative penalty the suppression of parishes, etc.,[44] indicates that suppression in general is to be considered in the nature of vindicative penalty, provided, of course, that it was decreed because of some public harm or detriment occasioned for the community. Therefore, in this case the suppression of a society by a decree of the ordinary would have no effect while recourse was pending, *i. e.*, such a recourse would be suspensive in its effect against the decree. For the same reasons also recourse against the penal threat of suppression or against the precept inherent in that threat is likewise suspensive in its effect.

2. *Lay Societies.* There does not seem to be any reason why the above principles cannot be applied also to lay societies. However some restriction must be made in regard to recourse against dismissal from a society. A lay society, having no recognition in Church law, cannot be made a defendant in a suit, even to remedy an injustice. The sphere of lay society's recognition can extend no farther than the recognition which is accorded to the individuals who compose that society. Being a private society, it has the privilege to accept or to exclude, to admit or to expel, members at will. There could be no recourse then, against dismissal, unless the dismissal was the result or the cause of some injustice. Recourse then would be tantamount to legal action against the injustice and not against the dismissal proper. And the action would then be, not against the society as such, but against the person or persons guilty.

The right of recourse against a decree of suppression enjoys somewhat greater latitude. The right to form a society is a natural right. The suppression of a society may in given cases imply the suppression of a natural right. The society, that is, the individual members, can have recourse to higher authority if they are hindered in the enjoyment of their natural right of forming a society. In accordance with the principles given in regard to the suppression of an ecclesiastical association, the immediate result of the recourse is (1) ***non-suspensive*** in character, if the society be suppressed for contentious reasons, and (2) ***suspensive*** in character, if the suppression is in the

[44] Canons 2291, 3° and 2292.

nature of a vindicative penalty. This latter case includes also the penal threat of suppression and the precept inherent in that threat.

In the treatment of recourse and appeal, the dismissal of a member and the suppression of a society were considered, inasmuch as these two factors could more frequently than others involve the question of recourse and appeal. However, any decree or sentence admits of recourse or appeal unless such action is denied by law.[45] If any decree or sentence other than that of dismissal or suppression is inflicted upon a member or upon a lay society recourse or appeal is allowed. The juridic effect of such a recourse or appeal is deducible from the principles which govern recourse or appeal from the decree or sentence of dismissal or suppression.

[45] Even when recourse and appeal are denied, the Code allows some extraordinary remedies to safeguard against injustice. Cf. canons 1879-1907.

CHAPTER X

CESSATION AND SUPPRESSION

ARTICLE 1. CESSATION OF A SOCIETY

A. *Non-incorporated Societies*

(a) *By lapse of time or purpose.* It stands to reason that if a society was founded only for a definite period of time, the society is dissolved by the lapse of that time. Likewise a society founded for a special purpose, *e. g.*, to perform some special work of charity during the time of war, will also cease with the disappearance of that end. However, since a lay society is a free union of the faithful, the time could be extended or the end altered, and thus the society could continue in existence. Excepted are incorporated societies which would have to have their charters renewed or extended. In all other cases the dissolution depends upon the will of the members. This is always true in an unincorporated lay society.

(b) *By the will of the members.* Just as a society is formed at the will of the members, so also it can be dissolved in the same manner, provided it does not exist through a formal decree of erection.[1] Unanimous consent would always dissolve the society, but a majority consent may or may not, depending upon the statutes. When a society is formed, statutes are drawn up to determine the end, to designate the means of attaining the end, and, in general, to reflect the make-up or constitution of the society, stabilizing, to a certain extent, its very existence. If the statutes, which were approved by the members at the institution of the society, demand a relative, an absolute, or a two-thirds majority vote, then the dissolution of the society is determined by that majority. In the absence of statutes or such regulations a mere relative or even absolute majority would not effect the dissolution of the society. For since two or three persons can form a society, the same number could also

[1] Schaefer, *De Religiosis*, n. 628.

continue its existence. One person alone could never do so except in the case of an incorporated society.

B. *Incorporated Societies*

1. *Ecclesiastical moral persons.* An ecclesiastical moral person is dissolved not only by suppression but also by the lapse of one hundred years after it has ceased to function as a society.[2] This is a privilege granted exclusively to church corporations. If, therefore, all but one member of a corporation dies or withdraws, the corporation continues to exist. If that last member dies, or discontinues the work of the society, the corporation continues to exist legally or canonically until the lapse of one hundred years from the time the work of the society ceased. But if any member's rights and obligations passed to his heir or successor, the corporation would continue to exist until the lapse of the one hundred years as stated above.[3] If a parish church, therefore, was destroyed and never rebuilt, the parish would still exist canonically for one hundred years, apart from a decree of suppression by the legitimate ecclesiastical authority.

Since an ecclesiastical association is formed into a moral person only through a decree of the legitimate ecclesiastical authority it can be suppressed within the one hundred years existence granted it by law only through suppression by the same legitimate authority. If therefore the members voted for dissolution this vote would not have any juridic effect until confirmed by the proper authority. Likewise, if the powers granted it are misused or abused the status of the association is not changed unless it was erected conditionally. Misuse or abuse of its powers would not cause its legal dissolution but would furnish grounds upon which the proper ecclesiastical authority could suppress it.

2. *Civil corporations.* In civil law, likewise, one member alone can function in accordance with the corporate rights of the society of which he alone remains a member. Heirs and successors of the

[2] Canon 102, § 1.

[3] Jone, *Gesetzbuch des kanonischen Rechtes,* under canon 102.

members of a corporation inherit their corporate powers.[4] The corporation does not cease therefore with the withdrawal or death of its members. It does cease, however, principally in the following ways:

(a) *Forfeiture of charter.* Since a charter of incorporation is a compact or contract between the members and the State, the State can bring proceedings to forfeit the charter [5] if the powers granted therein are not used,[6] if they are misused or abused,[7] or if the corporation itself is insolvent.[8] Sometimes an *ipso facto* operative forfeiture clause is contained in the charter and is thereby self-executing.

(b) *Repeal.* The right to repeal a charter of incorporation is sometimes retained by the State.[9]

(c) *Surrender of charter.* This can be done at the will of the members, but in order to be effective the surrender must be accepted by the State.[10]

(d) *Expiration of time.* If a charter was granted only for a period of time, the corporation is *ipso facto* dissolved at the expiration of that time without any direct action on the part of the members or the State.[11] The time required for the dissolution of a corporation after it has ceased to function depends upon statutory law. However, the State can in such cases bring proceedings to forfeit the charter.

Article 2. Suppression of Societies

A. *Ecclesiastical Societies*

Only he who has the right to erect associations can also suppress

[4] Dartmouth College v. Woodward, 4 Wheat. (U. S.), 518.

[5] Because of the pact between the members and the State, only the State has the right to bring these proceedings. Cf. Heard v. Talbot, 7 Gray (Mass.), 113.

[6] State v. Delmar Jockey, 200 Mo., 34.

[7] People v. North River Sugar Refining Co., 121 N. Y., 582.

[8] Holman v. State, 105 Ind., 569.

[9] Pomeroy, *Business Law*, p. 592.

[10] Boston Glass Mfg. v. Langdon, 24 Pick. (Mass.), 49.

[11] Clark v. American Cannel Coal Co., 165 Ind., 213.

them.[12] This power lies in the local ordinary who for some grave cause and with a proper safeguard of the right of recourse to the Holy See [13] can suppress even those associations which are erected by religious.[14] He cannot, however, suppress associations which have been erected by the Holy See.[15] What the just causes are will be discussed in the suppression of lay societies for the same causes can be applied to both ecclesiastical and lay societies. But it will be noted that the Code gives the power of suppression to local ordinaries only in respect to those societies which he has erected or approved either explicitly or implicitly.[16] What is said in regard to lay societies, the kinds of suppression, the just causes required, and the effects of suppression, can also be applied to ecclesiastical associations. But the administrative powers given to the pastor must be denied him in the suppression of ecclesiastical associations, inasmuch as competency for this matter resides exclusively in the local ordinary. It may be added also that the civil authority has no power in suppressing ecclesiastical associations.[17]

B. *Lay Societies*

Suppression can be effected either through a judicial or through an administrative process. In the present instance suppression through a judicial process needs no consideration. Its rarity makes its consideration impractical and, furthermore, what is said of suppression through an administrative process can be applied to it. Hence suppression by means of an administrative process will alone be considered.

Although the Code gives the ordinary no express power to suppress lay societies, he does have this power both by reason of his jurisdiction and by reason of pastoral office. Suppression because of

[12] Canon 699; S. C. C., *Spalaten.*, 14 dec. 1889, 25 ian. 1890—*ASS*, XXII (1890), 585; *Fontes*, n. 4276; S. C. C., *Liburnen.*, 7 sept. 1895—*ASS*, XXVIII (1895-1896), 496; *Fontes*, n. 4296; S. C. Consist., decr. 5 maii 1914—*AAS*, VI (1914), 312; De Meester, *Compendium*, n. 1080.

[13] Cf. *supra*, pp. 109-110.

[14] Canons 699 and 686, § 3; cf. Vromant, *op. cit.*, pp. 56-59.

[15] Canon 699, § 2.

[16] Canon 686.

[17] Vromant, *op. cit.*, p. 57, footnote 3.

some act on the part of the members of a lay society which act partakes of the nature of a crime is called *penal suppression,* while suppression because of a conflict or usurpation of rights is called *contentious suppression.*[18] Inasmuch as the pastor has the care of souls attached to his office he also is competent in this latter case.

(a) *Penal Suppression.* Since the inflicting of penalties is an act of jurisdiction which the pastor cannot exercise in the external forum,[19] the penal suppression of lay societies is reserved to the local ordinary. Inasmuch as in this case the act of suppression is considered to be a penalty, grave causes are necessary. A vindicative penalty tends directly to the expiation of a crime and the restoration of the public order.[20] Hence, this penalty cannot be applied unless the members of a society perpetrated some act which partook of the nature of a crime, that is, of the nature of a morally imputable, external, and grave violation of a law or precept [21] whereby public order was disturbed. This does not mean that any or all of the members sin thereby. Even though the act is not morally imputable to any particular member, it suffices that the society as a society commits the act. Less is required, then, for inflicting a vindicative penalty upon a society than upon individuals, for what is a grave cause as demanded by the Code for the suppression of societies is not necessarily a grave sin for the individual members or not even a grave sin for the society which is incapable of human acts.

Among the just causes for penal suppression are the following:

1. *Crime.* This is a general cause and may include any of the following although none of the following causes need strictly to imply the presence of a crime.

2. *Scandal.* A *crime* may be accompanied with scandal. The means which a society uses to raise money, *e. g.*, games of chance, gambling, etc., or the admission of forbidden members, or anything else even though harmless in itself, if it be the occasion of scandal to others, constitutes a grave cause.

[18] Cf. *supra,* p. 110, wherein it is shown that penal suppression partakes of the nature of a vindicative penalty. Cf. also *infra,* pp. 121-122.

[19] Cf. *supra,* p. 86.

[20] Canon 2286.

[21] Canon 2195.

3. *Loss or injury to others.* This cause could also be considered as possibly underlying a contentious suppression, but if it was serious or grave it could also be a cause for penal suppression, especially if it inflicted an injustice upon others.

4. *Rejection of ecclesiastical vigilance.* It is true that a lay society in the nature of a society is exempt from ecclesiastical supervision. If a society, therefore, refused to permit a priest to direct its activities or to govern it in any way, it could not solely for that reason be suppressed. But every individual is subject to the general vigilance of the Church. And to this lay societies also are subject. Though they do not have to subject themselves to the special vigilance of the Church, they are bound to subject themselves to its general vigilance. Anything pertaining to faith and morals, the laws of justice, etc., must be placed under ecclesiastical supervision. Failure to do so would constitute a just and grave cause punishable by suppression. To this classification must also be added the society's refusal to subject themselves to the special vigilance of the ordinary in those things which the law commits to his special care.[22]

5. *Other causes.* Any cause which constitutes a forbidden end and by the same token stands as a prohibition for the forming of a society with such an end in view also constitutes a cause for suppression. Among these are included secrecy, activities against public order, etc.[23]

(b) *Contentious suppression.*

1. *Competency of the local ordinary.* There can be no question of the local ordinary's competency to suppress societies. This right is derived not only from his threefold power of jurisdiction but from his pastoral office as well. He is the ordinary and immediate pastor of all the souls in the diocese committed to him.[24] This pastoral office gives him the right and the duty of the care of souls, of their sanctification and spiritual welfare, and of the fostering or the instituting of works of piety and charity. However, his right does not permit him to infringe upon the natural rights of others to form societies. It is

[22] Cf. *supra,* pp. 97-98.

[23] Cf. *supra,* pp. 47-48.

[24] Canon 334, § 1.

only when there is a conflict of rights that he can act. His right to suppress societies therefore, is limited to the conditions or causes to be explained later. But the exercise of this power is not in conflict with the rights of the pastor to whom he has committed the care of souls in a parish. The pastor's right is subordinate to the bishop's.

2. *Competency of the pastor.* The pastor must *ex officio* exercise the care of souls committed to him [25] from the moment he takes canonical possession of his parish.[26] This care of souls, as in the case of the bishop, besides the obligation of administering the sacraments, imposes the obligation of prudently correcting the erring and of bestowing paternal charity upon the poor, the sick, and the wretched.[27] The pastor must also promote the personal sanctification and the spiritual welfare of souls especially by fostering or instituting works of charity, faith, and piety.[28] These rights and duties of the pastor have been mentioned in regard to the ecclesiastical supervision of societies. They are repeated here to emphasize the exact pastoral rights and obligations concerning practically the whole spiritual life of a parish and any religious end which a society would undertake to attain.

It must be noted that a pastor is bound to foster or institute works of charity, faith, and piety. He is not bound to institute such works if they are already instituted. He has no right therefore to infringe upon the natural right of the faithful to form societies to accomplish these ends. He is bound to foster them unless, again, there is a conflict of rights. Then he has the right to suppress such societies for the reasons explained below.

To say that the pastor has no right whatever to suppress lay societies [29] is to deny him the fullness of his parochial power. He cannot proceed in a penal or judicial manner. In this he is but the *watchman* for the bishop. But the pastor is not devoid of all power. The very office which he holds gives him ordinary power of jurisdiction,

[25] Canon 464.

[26] Canon 461.

[27] Canon 467; Fanfani, *De Iure Parochorum*, nn. 209; 233.

[28] Canon 469; Fanfani, *op. cit.*, nn. 86; 341; 342; 343; cf. *supra*, pp. 88-89.

[29] *Contra* Schaaf, "Suppression of a Parish Lay Society," *American Ecclesiastical Review*, XCVI (1937), 301-306.

not indeed to make laws, render judgment in a formal manner, or to apply ecclesiastical penalties, but to govern his subjects nevertheless. This power may be compared to domestic power possessed by religious superiors who have no power of jurisdiction. But this power as it resides in the pastor is a participation of jurisdiction derived from the parochial office. Insofar as he is not restricted by law, the pastor can command and demand obedience in those things which are within his rights as well as in those things which concern the ministry and the running or administration of the parish. From this is deduced his right to suppress lay societies, provided that there is present a just and proportionate cause. This right the pastor can use in the contentious suppression of lay societies.

3. *Just causes for suppression.* The causes for which a pastor can lawfully suppress a lay society are based upon the conflict of rights. When the rights of his parishioners conflict with the rights of the pastor, those of the pastor, all things being equal, prevail. Therefore the following reasons give him the right to suppress a lay society:

(a) *The society's infringement upon the rights of the pastor.* Not every work of charity or of piety done by others infringes upon the pastor's rights. He is, on the contrary, bound to foster them. But some society in the exercise of such works may possibly benefit a few to the detriment of others. If the pastor thinks that another method or society would be more beneficial he can order the society suppressed. Being the pastor to whom the care of souls has been committed, he has the right to foster or institute whatever methods are most beneficial to his parish as a whole. This is an exercise of his domestic power inasmuch as it is an act of parochial administration.

(b) *The society's duplication of the aim of an extant society.* This is closely related to the cause above noted and can be identical with it. However it can differ in that the permission to allow two societies of the same nature to exist in the same parish does not necessarily hinder works of piety and charity. But the one society may prove a hindrance to the other. Because of this injury it may be suppressed. Moreover, the existence of two identical societies in the same place, as also the unnecessary multiplication of societies, is contrary to the mind of the Church as is seen both from the history of societies and from the present legislation on ecclesiastical societies.

Suppression in this case is likewise an exercise of domestic power inasmuch as it is an act of administration.

It has been said that the pastor has the right in the above cases to suppress a lay society. He has no power over ecclesiastical societies unless the bishop has delegated it to him. He has also no power to suppress lay societies if the suppression is the result of some act which shares the nature of a crime. But he does have administrative or domestic power to suppress lay societies if there is a conflict of its rights with his rights, or if harm is done to other societies. Expedience may dictate that instead of ordering a society suppressed he should simply discourage it, *e. g.*, by refusing to allow it to raise money, by denying it a meeting place, etc.,[30] but it cannot be admitted that he has no right to suppress it. Nor can it be admitted that the society does not have to obey. It does however have the right of recourse to the local ordinary or to higher ecclesiastical authority.[31]

The power of suppressing lay societies can be extended to other priest's only in so far as they possess the pastoral office and act in an administrative manner. The extent of their possession of the pastoral office when they are not vested with the title of pastor has been seen previously.[32] In general, the dean, a substitute pastor, and parochial assistants have no right to suppress societies. For grave reasons the power can be extended to administrators and acting vicars.

Article 3. The Effects of Suppression

A. *Dissolution*

By suppression a society is completely dissolved. The right to form a society, however, is not taken from the members. That is a natural right that they always enjoy if they are not otherwise impeded. Therefore a new society can be formed with a different end, or with different means to attain the same end, depending upon the causes of suppression. But the society as it existed before suppression

[30] Schaaf, "Suppression of a Parish Society," *AER*, XCVI (1937), 306.
[31] Cf. *supra*, pp. 112-113.
[32] Cf. *supra*, pp. 90-91.

cannot again be formed until the cessation of the causes on account of which it was suppressed. The causes having ceased the society can again be formed.

B. *Rights and Obligations of Members*

The rights of the members of a suppressed society cease with the society, provided that these rights were derived from membership in the society. The obligations contracted by the society, however, remain. That is, any debts contracted by the society must be met by the members. Legally the society itself is not bound if it is not incorporated. But debts and other obligations, because of the legal non-existence of the society, bind him who legally contracted them. However the moral law demands that each one who was a member of a suppressed lay society fulfill its obligations in a just proportion. The suppression of a society does not excuse from the fulfillment of the laws of justice.

C. *Temporal Goods*

The temporal goods of a suppressed ecclesiastical moral person become the property of the immediately superior ecclesiastical moral person, proper regard being given to the will of the donor and the obligations of the association.[33] The goods of an ecclesiastical association not erected as a moral person remain with the members.[34] Hence it can be divided proportionately among the members. The same is true also of lay societies. Since ownership rests with the members and not with the society itself, if then the society is dissolved, the goods must be divided proportionately after all debts and obligations are fulfilled.[35] However, money or property which is given to a society with some unfulfilled attached condition must be returned, for the ownership was not transferred as long as the condition was not fulfilled. But what the society or the members possessed or owned in common should be distributed equitably among the members of a suppressed lay society.

[33] Canon 1501.

[34] Schaefer, *De Religiosis*, n. 628.

[35] Jone, *Gesetzbuch des kanonischen Rechtes*, under canon 99.

Civil law, as a rule, makes no regulation in regard to the goods or property of a corporation except with regard to the matter of distribution after the dissolution of the corporation and the fulfillment of all obligations. Any other arrangement would have to be specified in the charter. Some public utility corporations could by statute have other stipulations placed upon the distribution of the property, but a lay society can of course not be classified as a public utility. *A fortiori* the civil law would not legislate concerning a distribution of the goods of an unincorporated private lay society, for legally the law cannot advert to its existence for the reason that it is not recognized by the law as existent. The civil law would, however, take cognizance of property held in trust even by an unincorporated lay society, holding responsible the person who was last known to have possession of the fund.

CONCLUSIONS

Within the foregoing pages the subject of lay societies has been discussed both as to its historical development and as to its present canonical status. Very little has been written about lay societies since the promulgation of the Code. Hence their status was determined by the Church law on ecclesiastical associations in as far as that law is applicable to lay societies and by the general laws of the Church. Gathered here in summary are the most particular conclusions reached in the course of this study:

1. In its constitution and make-up a lay society should conform itself to the law of the Church in as far as it is possible and in as far as it is convenient for its successful operation.

2. Anyone not forbidden by the common law of the Church or the status of the society can become a member. This includes non-Catholics in as far as they are not otherwise impeded or forbidden, and minors who have reached the age of fourteen if the society is of a purely spiritual nature.

3. Admission into a society implies a quasi-contract. Both admission and renunciation of membership presuppose consent from both the member and the society.

4. The temporal goods of a lay society belong, according to the natural law, to the society. However, both canonically and legally the title of ownership can reside only in some one who possesses juridic personality, unless the society is incorporated in civil law, in which case it receives juridic personality, but only in civil law.

5. The administration of the goods of a lay society is exempt from all ecclesiastical supervision. The money or property constitutes a private fund and, therefore, in no way belongs to the Church, to the pastor, or to the parish, and cannot be appropriated without the society's consent.

6. Lay societies are not bound by the special laws of the Church on societies. They are, however, subject to the general vigilance of both the local ordinary and the pastor in so far as each one of the faithful is individually subject especially in matters of faith and

morals and the laws of justice. They are subject also to the special vigilance of the local ordinary in those things that are especially committed to his care.

7. Diocesan control of lay societies is contrary to the mind of the Church and the spirit of her laws. Diocesan unions of societies, however, are not contrary to the law, as long as they are simply an aid to the well-being of parish societies, but they cannot lawfully undertake to rule or dominate the activities of parochial units.

8. Resource against dismissal from a lay society is tantamount to a legal action against an injustice. Recourse against a decree of suppression suspends the execution of the decree if it was inflicted as a vindicative penalty, that is, if suppression is *penal.* If suppression is *contentious,* the execution of the decree is not suspended.

9. The pastor as well as the local ordinary is competent in the *contentious* suppression of lay societies, but only the local ordinary is competent in the *penal* suppression of such societies.

10. The goods of dissolved or suppressed lay societies must be distributed proportionately among the members, due consideration being given to the prescripts of the statutes and to any trust fund established for specific purposes. While there is no legal obligation for the society as such to fulfill its obligations, yet the natural and moral law continue to bind the members of a dissolved society.

BIBLIOGRAPHY

Sources

Acta Apostolicae Sedis, Commentarium Officiale, Romae, 1909—

Acta et Decreta Concilii Plenarii Baltimorensis Tertii, A. D. MDCCCLXXXIV, Baltimorae, John Murphy, 1886.

Acta et Decreta Sacrorum Conciliorum Recentiorum, Collectio Lacensis, 7 vols., Friburgi Brisgoviae, 1870-1890.

Acta Sanctae Sedis, 41 vols., Romae, 1865-1908.

Bullarii Romani Continuatio Summorum Pontificum, 19 vols., Prato, 1757-1883, II, *Benedicti XIV Bullarium* (1846).

Bullarum Diplomatum et Privilegiorum Sanctorum Romanorum Pontificum Taurinensis Editio, 24 vols. et Appendix, Neapoli, 1857-1872.

Codex Iuris Canonici Pii X Pontificis Maximi Iussu digestus, Benedicti Papae XV auctoritate promulgatus, Romae: Typis Polyglottis Vaticanis, 1917; Reimpressio, 1933.

Codicis Iuris Canonici Fontes cura Emi. Petri Card. Gasparri editi, 9 vols., Romae (postea Civitate Vaticana): Typis Polyglottis Vaticanis, 1923-1939. (Vols. VII-IX ed. cura et studio Emi. Iustiniani Card. Serédi.)

Concilia Provincialia Baltimori habita ab anno 1829 usque ad annum 1849 (2. ed., Baltimori: Joannis Murphy et Socii, 1851).

Concilii Plenarii Baltimorensis II, in Ecclesia Metropolitana Baltimorensi, a die VII ad diem XXI Octobris, A. D. MDCCCLXVI, habiti, et a Sede Apostolica Recogniti, Acta et Decreta, Baltimorae, John Murphy, 1868.

Concilium Plenarium Totius Americae Septentrionalis Foederatae, Baltimori habitum anno 1852, Baltimori: Joannis Murphy et Socii, 1853.

Corpus Iuris Civilis, 3 vols., Berolini: apud Weidmannos, 1928-1929. Vol. I, ed. stereotypa quinta decima, *Institutiones*,—Paulus Krueger; *Digesta*,—Theodorus Mommsen, retractavit Paulus Krueger; Vol. II, ed. stereotypa decima, *Codex Iustinianus*,—Paulus Krueger; Vol. III, et stereotypa quinta, *Novellae*,—Rudolphus Schoell; opus Schoellii morte interceptum absolvit Guilelmus Kroll.

Decreta Authentica Sacrae Congregationis Indulgentiis Sacrisque Reliquiis praepositae (1668-1882) iussu et auctoritate Leonis XIII edita, Romae: Ratisbonae, 1883.

Decretum Gratiani emendatum et notationibus illustratum una cum glossis Gregorii XIII, Pont. Max., iussu editum, Romae, 1582.

Hardouin, Jean, *Acta Conciliorum et Epistolae Decretales ac Constitutiones Summorum Pontificum*, 12 vols., Parisiis, 1715.

Mansi, Joannes Dominicus, *Sacrorum Conciliorum Nova et Amplissima Collectio*, 53 vols. in 59, Paris-Leipzig-Arnhem, 1901-1927.

Monumenta Germaniae Historica, 188 vols. incomplete, 1826—

Epistolae Selectae, I, *S. Bonifatii et Lulli Epistolae*, ed. Michael Tangl, Berolini, 1916.

Leges (in folio), 5 vols., 1835-1889; Vol. I, *Capitularia Regum Francorum*, ed. Georgius Henricus Pertz, Hannoverae, 1863, Neudruck, 1925; Vol. III, *Leges Nationum Germanicarum*, ed. J. Merkel, 1863, Neudruck, 1925.

Leges (in quarto): *Legum Sectio I, Leges Nationum Germanicarum*, Tom. I, *Leges Visigothorum*, ed. K. Zeumer, 1902; *Legum Sectio III, Concilia*, Tom. II, recensivit Albertus Werminghoff, 1893.

Scriptores, XIII, ed. G. Waitz, Hannoverae, 1881.

Sacri Concilii Tridentini Canones et Decreta, Coloniae Agrippinae, 1621.

Authors

Aichner, Simon, *Compendium Iuris Canonici*, Brixinae, 1887.

———, *Compendium Iuris Ecclesiastici*, Brixinae, 1900.

[Bachofen], Charles Augustine, *A Commentary on the New Code of Canon Law*, 8 vols. (Vol. II, 6. ed., 1936; Vol. IV, 3. ed., 1925; Vol. V, 5. ed., 1935), St. Louis-London: Herder.

Bartlett, Chester J., *The Tenure of Parochial Property in the United States of America*, The Catholic University of America Canon Law Studies, n. 31, Washington, D. C.: The Catholic University of America, 1926.

Bassi, John Baptist, *Tractatus de Sodalitiis*, Romae, 1725.

Beil, Josef, *Das kirchliche Vereinsrecht*, Paderborn: Schöningh, 1932.

Benedictus XIV, *De Synodo Dioecesana*, 2 vols., Parmae, 1764.

Beringer, Franz, *Die Ablässe, ihr Wesen und Gebrauch*, bearbeitet von A. Steinen, 2 vols., Paderborn: Schöningh, 1921-1922.

Beste, Udalricus, *Introductio in Codicem*, Collegeville, Minn.: St. John's Abbey Press, 1938.

Blackstone, William, *Commentaries on the Laws of England*, edited by Thomas M. Cooley, Chicago: Callaghan, 1876.

Blat, Alberto, *Commentarium Textus Codicis Iuris Canonici*, 6 vols., Romae: Collegio "Angelico," 1921-1927.

Borkowski, Aurelius L., *De Confraternitatibus Ecclesiasticis*, Washingtonii: Universitas Catholica Americae, 1918.

Bouix, D., *Tractatus de Episcopis*, Paris, 1859.

Brown, Brendan F., *The Canonical Juristic Personality with Special Reference to Its Status in the United States of America*, The Catholic University of America Canon Law Studies, n. 39, Washington, D. C.: The Catholic University of America, 1927.

Cappello, F. M., *Tractatus Canonico-Moralis de Sacramentis*, Vol. I, 3. ed., Romae: Marietti, 1938.

Cavagnis, Felix, *Institutiones Iuris Publici Ecclesiastici*, 3 vols., 4. ed., Romae, 1906.

Chelodi, Joannis, *Ius Poenale et Ordo Procedendi in Iudiciis Criminalibus*, 4. ed., by Vigilius Dalpiaz, Tridenti: Ardesi, 1935.

Cicognani, Hamletus I., *Commentarium in Librum I Codicis*, Romae: ex Schola Typographica "Pio X," 1925.

Coady, John Joseph, *The Appointment of Pastors*, The Catholic University of America Canon Law Studies, n. 52, Washington, D. C.: The Catholic University of America, 1929.

Cocchi, G., *Commentarium in Codicem Iuris Canonici ad Usum Scholarum*, 5 vols. in 8, Vols. III-VII, 3. ed., Vols. II et VIII, 4. ed., Vol. I, 5. ed., Augustae Taurinorum: Marietti, 1931-1938.

Connolly, Thomas A., *Appeals*, The Catholic University of America Canon Law Studies, n. 79, Washington, D. C.: The Catholic University of America, 1932.

Coronata, Matthaeus Conte a, *Institutiones Iuris Canonici*, 5 vols., Taurini: Marietti, Vols. I et II, 2. ed., 1939; Vol. III, 1933; Vol. IV, 1935; Vol. V, 1936.

———, *De Locis et Temporibus Sacris*, Augustae Taurinorum: Marietti, 1922.

De Meester, A., *Juris Canonici et Juris Canonico-Civilis Compendium*, nova ed., 3 vols. in 4, Brugis: Desclée, De Brouwer & Si, 1921-1928.

Dignan, Patrick J., *A History of the Legal Incorporation of Catholic Church Property in the United States (1784-1932)*, Washington, D. C.: The Catholic University of America, 1933.

Doheny, William J., *Practical Problems in Church Finance*, Milwaukee: Bruce, 1941.

Ebner, Adalbert, *Die klösterlichen Gebetsverbrüderungen*, Regensburg, 1890.

Eichmann, Eduard, *Lehrbuch des Kirchenrechts auf Grund des Codex Iuris Canonici*, 2. ed., Paderborn: Schöningh, 1926.

Esswein, Anthony A., *Extrajudicial Penal Powers of Ecclesiastical Superiors*, The Catholic University of America Canon Law Studies, n. 127, Washington, D. C.: The Catholic University of America Press, 1941.

Fanfani, Ludovicus, *De Iure Parochorum*, altera editio, Taurini: Marietti, 1936.

Ferraris, F. Lucius, *Prompta Bibliotheca Canonica, Iuridica, Moralis, Theologica, necnon Ascetica, Polemica, Rubricistica, Historica*, 9 vols., Romae, 1885-1899: Vol. IX ed. Bucceroni.

Greteman, Francis H., *Pious Societies in Canon Law*, Licentiate Dissertation, Washington, D. C.: The Catholic University of America, 1937.

Goyeneche, S., *Iuris Canonici Summa Principia, Partes II (De Religiosis) et III (De Laicis) Libri II Codicis*, Romae: Tip. Pol. "Cuore di Maria," 1938.

Guilday, Peter, *A History of the Councils of Baltimore*, New York: Macmillan, 1932.

Hannan, Jerome D., *The Canon Law of Wills*, The Catholic University of America Canon Law Studies, n. 86, Washington, D. C.: The Catholic University of America, 1934.

Harbrecht, Joseph J., *The Lay Apostolate*, St. Louis: Herder, 1929.

Heston, Edward L., *The Alienation of Church Property in the United States*, The Catholic University of America Canon Law Studies, n. 132, Washington, D. C.: The Catholic University of America Press, 1941.

Jone, Heribert, *Gesetzbuch des kanonischen Rechtes*, 3 vols., Paderborn: Schöningh, 1939-1941.

Lambert, J. Malet, *Two Thousand Years of Gild Life*, Hull, 1891.

Lega, Michael, *Praelectiones in Textum Iuris Canonici—De Delictis et Poenis*, 2. ed., Romae, 1910.

———, *De Iudiciis Ecclesiasticis*, Vol. I, 3. ed., Romae, 1905.

Loening, Edgar, *Geschichte des Deutschen Kirchenrechts*, 2 vols., Strassburg, 1878.

Lydon, P. J., *Ready Answers in Canon Law*, New York-Cincinnati-Chicago-San Francisco: Benziger Brothers, 1934.

Maroto, P., *Institutiones Iuris Canonici ad Normam Novi Codicis*, 2 vols., Madrid, 1919.

Michael, Emil, *Geschichte des deutschen Volkes*, 3 vols., Freiburg im Breisgau, 1897-1903.

Michiels, Gommarus, *Normae Generales Iuris Canonici*, 2 vols., Lublin-Polonia: Universitas Catholica, 1929.

———, *De Delictis et Poenis*, Lublin-Polonia, 1934.

Migne, Jacques Paul, *Patrologiae Cursus Completus, Series Latina*, 221 vols., Parisiis, 1844-1864.

Muratori, L. A., *Antiquitates Italicae Medii Aevi*, 6 vols., Mediolani, 1738-1743.

Murphy, Charles K., *The Spirit of the Society of St. Vincent de Paul*, London, Longmans, Green & Co., 1940.

Noldin, H.-Schmitt, A., *Summa Theologiae Moralis*, 26. ed., 3 vols., Oeniponte: Rauch, 1938-1939; Vol. III, *De Sacramentis*.

Ojetti, Benedictus, *Commentarium in Codicem Iuris Canonici*, 4 vols., Romae: Apud Aedes Universitatis Gregorianae, 1927-1931.

Ottaviani, Alaphridus, *Institutiones Iuris Publici Ecclesiastici*, 2. ed., 2 vols., E Civitate Vaticana: Typis Polyglottis Vaticanis, 1936.

Pomeroy, Dwight A., *Business Law*, Cincinnati: South-Western Publishing Co., 1931.

Prümmer, Dominicus M., *Manuale Iuris Canonici*, 4. et 5. ed., Friburgi Brisgoviae: Herder, 1927.

Quigley, Joseph, *Condemned Societies*, The Catholic University of America Canon Law Studies, n. 46, Washington, D. C.: The Catholic University of America, 1927.

Reiffenstuel, A., *Ius Canonicum Universum*, 5 vols. in 7, Parisiis, 1864-1870.

Roberti, Franciscus, *De Delictis et Poenis*, Vol. I, Pars I, Romae: Apud Aedes Facultates Iuridicae ad S. Apollinaris, 1938.

Ryan, Gerald Aloysius, *Principles of Episcopal Jurisdiction*, The Catholic University of America Canon Law Studies, n. 120, Washington, D. C.: The Catholic University of America Press, 1939.

Sägmüller, J. B., *Lehrbuch des katholischen Kirchenrechts,* 3. ed., 2 vols., Freiburg im Breisgau, 1914.

Schaefer, Timotheus, *De Religiosis ad Normam Codicis Iuris Canonici,* 3. ed., Romae: Typis Polyglottis Vaticanis, 1940.

Schmalzgrueber, Franciscus, *Ius Ecclesiasticum Universum,* 5 vols. in 12, Romae, 1843-1845.

Schulze, F., *Manual of Pastoral Theology,* 3. ed., St. Louis: B. Herder Book Co., 1923.

Smith, Toulmin, *English Gilds,* with a preliminary essay in five parts on *The History and Development of Gilds* by Lujo Brentano, London, 1870.

Swoboda, Innocent, *Ignorance in Relation to the Imputability of Delicts,* The Catholic University of America Canon Law Studies, n. 143, Washington, D. C.: The Catholic University of America Press, 1941.

Tarquini, Camillus, *Iuris Ecclesiastici Publici Institutiones,* Romae, 1862.

Trade Gilds of Europe, "United States Consular Reports," Washington, D. C.: Government Printing Office, 1885.

Van Hove, Alphonsus, *Commentarium Lovaniense in Codicem Iuris Canonici,* Vol. I, Tom. II, *De Legibus Ecclesiasticis,* Mechliniae: H. Dessain, 1930.

Vermeersch, A.-Creusen, J., *Epitome Iuris Canonici,* 3 vols., Mechliniae, Vol. I, 6. ed., 1937; Vol. II, 5. ed., 1936; Vol. III, 6. ed., 1940.

Vromant, G., *De Fidelium Associationibus,* Louvain: Museum Lessianum, 1932.

Weber, G. Anton, *Die Römischen Katakomben,* Regensburg, 1906.

Wernz, F.-Vidal, P., *Ius Canonicum,* 7 toms. in 8 vols., Romae: Apud Aedes Universitatis Gregorianae, 1923-1938.

Woerner, J., *American Law of Administration,* 2. ed., Boston, 1899.

Woywood, Stanislaus, *A Practical Commentary on the Code of Canon Law,* 4. ed., 2 vols., New York: Wagner, 1932.

Zollman, Carl, *American Church Law,* St. Paul: West Publishing Co., 1933.

Periodicals

American Ecclesiastical Review (AER), Philadelphia, 1889—

Annales Ecclesiasticae, Romae, 1893-1911.

Apollinaris, Romae, 1928—

Catholic Historical Review, Washington, 1915.

Commentarium pro Religiosis (later, *Commentarium pro Religiosis et Missionariis*), Romae, 1920—

Il Dirrito Ecclesiastico, Romae, 1890—

Il Monitore Ecclesiastico, Romae, 1876—

Jurist, The, Washington, 1941—

Revue d'Histoire Ecclesiastique, Louvain, 1900—

Articles

Anonymous, "Altar Societies," *AER,* XCII (1935), 421.

———, "Catholic Instruction League," *AER,* XCI (1934), 73-75.

———, "Organization of Catholic Laymen," *AER*, LXXVI (1927), 442-444.

———, "Pastor's Jurisdiction Over Parish Societies," *AER*, LXXXVII (1932), 307-311.

———, "Patriotic Association in Religion," *AER*, LXXVI (1927), 537-539.

Donovan, Jos. P., "Is This the Long Looked for Church Society: The Legion of Mary," *AER*, LXXXVI (1932), 244-259.

Garesché, Edward, "The Sodality Spirit," *AER*, LXVIII (1923), 479-487.

McGrath, Owen, "Catholic Action's Big Opportunity," *AER*, XCI (1934), 280-287.

Schaaf, "Suppression of a Parish Society," *AER*, XCVI (1937), 301-306.

White, Robert J., "Certain Aspects of the Legal Status of the Church in the United States," *The Jurist*, I (1941), 20-49.

ABBREVIATIONS

AAS—*Acta Apostolicae Sedis.*
AER—*The American Ecclesiastical Review.*
Art.—Article.
ASS—*Acta Sanctae Sedis.*
C—Codex (Justinianus).
Ch.—Chapter.
Coll. Lac.—*Collectio Lacensis.*
C. Th.—Codex Theodosianus.
D.—Digest.
Decr. Auth.—*Decreta Authentica* (S. C. Indulg.).
Fontes—*Codicis Iuris Canonici Fontes cura . . . Gasparri editi.*
Ibid.—(*Ibidem*) The preceding reference.
Loc. cit.—*Loco citato.*
Mansi—*Sacrorum Conciliorum Nova et Amplissima Collectio.*
MGH—*Monumenta Germaniae Historica.*
MPL—Migne, *Patrologia Latina.*
N.—Novellae (Justinianae).
Op. cit.—*Opere citato.*
S. C. C.—Sacra Congregatio Concilii.
S. C. Consist.—Sacra Congregatio Consistorialis.
S. C. Ep. et Reg.—Sacra Congregatio Episcoporum et Regularium.
S. C. Indulg.—Sacra Congregatio Indulgentiarum.
S. C. P. F.—Sacra Congregatio de Propaganda Fide.
S. C. S. Off.—Sacra Congregatio Sancti Officii.

ALPHABETICAL INDEX

BIOGRAPHICAL NOTE

THOMAS JAMES CLARKE was born September 29, 1908, in Indianapolis, Indiana. He received his elementary and secondary education in the Catholic schools in that city. After two years in Cathedral High School he entered St. Meinrad's Seminary where he completed his philosophical and theological courses. He was ordained on May 22, 1934. The following six years he spent as assistant pastor at St. Anthony's Church in Evansville, Indiana. In September, 1940, he enrolled in the School of Canon Law at the Catholic University of America, where he received the degree of Baccalaureate in Canon Law in June, 1941, and the degree of Licentiate in Canon Law in May, 1942.

CANON LAW STUDIES *

1. Freriks, Rev. Celestine A., C.PP.S., J.C.D., Religious Congregations in Their External Relations, 121 pp., 1916.
2. Galliher, Rev. Daniel M., O.P., J.C.D., Canonical Elections, 117 pp., 1917.
3. Borkowski, Rev. Aurelius L., O.F.M., J.C.D., De Confraternitatibus Ecclesiasticis, 136 pp., 1918.
4. Castillo, Rev. Cayo, J.C.D., Disertacion Historico-Canonica sobre la Potestad del Cabildo en Sede Vacante o Impedida del Vicario Capitular, 99 pp., 1919 (1918).
5. Kubelbeck, Rev. William J., S.T.B., J.C.D., The Sacred Penitentiaria and Its Relation to Faculties of Ordinaries and Priests, 129 pp., 1918.
6. Petrovits, Rev. Joseph, J.C., S.T.D., J.C.D., The New Church Law on Matrimony, X-461 pp., 1919.
7. Hickey, Rev. John J., S.T.B., J.C.D., Irregularities and Simple Impediments in the New Code of Canon Law, 100 pp., 1920.
8. Klekotka, Rev. Peter J., S.T.B., J.C.D., Diocesan Consultors, 179 pp., 1920.
9. Wanenmacher, Rev. Francis, J.C.D., The Evidence in Ecclesiastical Procedure Affecting the Marriage Bond, 1920 (Printed 1935).
10. Golden, Rev. Henry Francis, J.C.D., Parochial Benefices in the New Code, IV-119 pp., 1921 (Printed 1925).
11. Koudelka, Rev. Charles J., J.C.D., Pastors, Their Rights and Duties According to the New Code of Canon Law, 211 pp., 1921.
12. Melo, Rev. Antonius, O.F.M., J.C.D., De Exemptione Regularium, X-188 pp., 1921.
13. Schaaf, Rev. Valentine Theodore, O.F.M., S.T.B., J.C.D., The Cloister, X-180 pp., 1921.
14. Burke, Rev. Thomas Joseph, S.T.D., J.C.D., Competence in Ecclesiastical Tribunals, IV-117 pp., 1922.
15. Leech, Rev. George Leo, J.C.D., A Comparative Study of the Constitution "Apostolicae Sedis" and the "Codex Juris Canonici," 179 pp., 1922.
16. Motry, Rev. Hubert Louis, S.T.D., J.C.D., Diocesan Faculties According to the Code of Canon Law, II-167 pp., 1922.
17. Murphy, Rev. George Lawrence, J.C.D., Delinquencies and Penalties in the Administration and the Reception of the Sacraments, IV-121 pp., 1923.
18. O'Reilly, Rev. John Anthony, S.T.B., J.C.D., Ecclesiastical Sepulture in the New Code of Canon Law, II-129 pp., 1923.

* Below n. 100 only the following numbers are still available: Nn. 3, 4, 9, 25, 34, 57 and 75. Beginning with n. 100 only the following are unavailable: Nn. 100, 101, 102, 104, 105, 107, 108, 109, 111 and 113.

19. MICHALICKA, REV. WENCESLAS CYRILL, O.S.B., J.C.D., Judicial Procedure in Dismissal of Clerical Exempt Religious, 107 pp., 1923.
20. DARGIN, REV. EDWARD VINCENT, S.T.B., J.C.D., Reserved Cases According to the Code of Canon Law, IV-103 pp., 1924.
21. GODFREY, REV. JOHN A., S.T.B., J.C.D., The Right of Patronage According to the Code of Canon Law, 153 pp., 1924.
22. HAGEDORN, REV. FRANCIS EDWARD, J.C.D., General Legislation on Indulgences, II-154 pp., 1924.
23. KING, REV. JAMES IGNATIUS, J.C.D., The Administration of the Sacraments to Dying Non-Catholics, V-141 pp., 1924.
24. WINSLOW, REV. FRANCIS JOSEPH, O.F.M., J.C.D., Vicars and Prefects Apostolic, IV-149 pp., 1924.
25. CORREA, REV. JOSE SERVELION, S.T.L., J.C.D., La Potestad Legislativa de la Iglesia Catolica, IV-127 pp., 1925.
26. DUGAN, REV. HENRY FRANCIS, A.M., J.C.D., The Judiciary Department of the Diocesan Curia, 87 pp., 1925.
27. KELLER, REV. CHARLES FREDERICK, S.T.B., J.C.D., Mass Stipends, 167 pp., 1925.
28. PASCHANG, REV. JOHN LINUS, J.C.D., The Sacramentals According to the Code of Canon Law, 129 pp., 1925.
29. PIONTEK, REV. CYRILLUS, O.F.M., S.T.B., J.C.D., De Indulto Exclaustrationis necnon Saecularizationis, XIII-289 pp., 1925.
30. KEARNEY, REV. RICHARD JOSEPH, S.T.B., J.C.D., Sponsors at Baptism According to the Code of Canon Law, IV-127 pp., 1925.
31. BARTLETT, REV. CHESTER JOSEPH, A.M., LL.B., J.C.D., The Tenure of Parochial Property in the United States of America, V-108 pp., 1926.
32. KILKER, REV. ADRIAN JEROME, J.C.D., Extreme Unction, V-425 pp., 1926.
33. MCCORMICK, REV. ROBERT EMMETT, J.C.D., Confessors of Religious, VIII-266 pp., 1926.
34. MILLER, REV. NEWTON THOMAS, J.C.D., Founded Masses According to the Code of Canon Law, VII-93 pp., 1926.
35. ROELKER, REV. EDWARD G., S.T.D., J.C.D., Principles of Privilege According to the Code of Canon Law, XI-166 pp., 1926.
36. BAKALARCZYK, REV. RICHARDUS, M.I.C., J.U.D., De Novitiatu, VIII-208 pp., 1927.
37. PIZZUTI, REV. LAWRENCE, O.F.M., J.U.L., De Parochis Religiosis, 1927. (Not Printed.)
38. BLILEY, REV. NICHOLAS MARTIN, O.S.B., J.C.D., Altars According to the Code of Canon Law, XIX-132 pp., 1927.
39. BROWN, MR. BRENDAN FRANCIS, A.B., LL.M., J.U.D., The Canonical Juristic Personality with Special Reference to its Status in the United States of America, V-212 pp., 1927.
40. CAVANAUGH, REV. WILLIAM THOMAS, C.P., J.U.D., The Reservation of the Blessed Sacrament, VIII-101 pp., 1927.

41. Doheny, Rev. William J., C.S.C., A.B., J.U.D., Church Property: Modes of Acquisition, X-118 pp., 1927.
42. Feldhaus, Rev. Aloysius H., C.PP.S., J.C.D., Oratories, IX-141 pp., 1927.
43. Kelly, Rev. James Patrick, A.B., J.C.D., The Jurisdiction of the Simple Confessor, X-208 pp., 1927.
44. Neuberger, Rev. Nicholas J., J.C.D., Canon 6 or the Relation of the Codex Juris Canonici to the Preceding Legislation, V-95 pp., 1927.
45. O'Keefe, Rev. Gerald Michael, J.C.D., Matrimonial Dispensations, Powers of Bishops, Priests, and Confessors, VIII-232 pp., 1927.
46. Quigley, Rev. Joseph A. M., A.B., J.C.D., Condemned Societies, 139 pp., 1927.
47. Zaplotnik, Rev. Johannes Leo, J.C.D., De Vicariis Foraneis, X-142 pp., 1927.
48. Duskie, Rev. John Aloysius, A.B., J.C.D., The Canonical Status of the Orientals in the United States, VIII-196 pp., 1928.
49. Hyland, Rev. Francis Edward, J.C.D., Excommunciation, Its Nature, Historical Development and Effects, VIII-181 pp., 1928.
50. Reinmann, Rev. Gerald Joseph, O.M.C., J.C.D., The Third Order Secular of Saint Francis, 201 pp., 1928.
51. Schenk, Rev. Francis J., J.C.D., The Matrimonial Impediments of Mixed Religion and Disparity of Cult, XVI-318 pp., 1929.
52. Coady, Rev. John Joseph, S.T.D., J.U.D., A.M., The Appointment of Pastors, VIII-150 pp., 1929.
53. Kay, Rev. Thomas Henry, J.C.D., Competence in Matrimonial Procedure, VIII-164 pp., 1929.
54. Turner, Rev. Sidney Joseph, C.P., J.U.D., The Vow of Poverty, XLIX-217 pp., 1929.
55. Kearney, Rev. Raymond A., A.B., S.T.D., J.C.D., The Principles of Delegation, VII-149 pp., 1929.
56. Conran, Rev. Edward James, A.B., J.C.D., The Interdict, V-163 pp., 1930.
57. O'Neill, Rev. William H., J.C.D., Papal Rescripts of Favor, VII-218 pp., 1930.
58. Bastnagel, Rev. Clement Vincent, J.U.D., The Appointment of Parochial Adjutants and Assistants, XV-257 pp., 1930.
59. Ferry, Rev. William A., A.B., J.C.D., Stole Fees, V-136 pp., 1930.
60. Costello, Rev. John Michael, A.B., J.C.D., Domicile and Quasi-Domicile, VII-201 pp., 1930.
61. Kremer, Rev. Michael Nicholas, A.B., S.T.B., J.C.D., Church Support in the United States, VI-136 pp., 1930.
62. Angulo, Rev. Luis, C.M., J.C.D., Legislation de la Iglesia sobre la intencion en la application de la Santa Misa, VII-104 pp., 1931.
63. Frey, Rev. Wolfgang Norbert, O.S.B., A.B., J.C.D., The Act of Religious Profession, VIII-174 pp., 1931.

64. ROBERTS, REV. JAMES BRENDAN, A.B., J.C.D., The Banns of Marriage, XIV-140 pp., 1931.
65. RYDER, REV. RAYMOND ALOYSIUS, A.B., J.C.D., Simony, IX-151 pp., 1931.
66. CAMPAGNA, REV. ANGELO, PH.D., J.U.D., Il Vicario Generale del Vescovo, VII-205 pp., 1931.
67. COX, REV. JOSEPH GODFREY, A.B., J.C.D., The Administration of Seminaries, VI-124 pp., 1931.
68. GREGORY, REV. DONALD J., J.U.D., The Pauline Privilege, XV-165 pp., 1931.
69. DONOHUE, REV. JOHN F., J.C.D., The Impediment of Crime, VII-110 pp., 1931.
70. DOOLEY, REV. EUGENE A., O.M.I., J.C.D., Church Law on Sacred Relics, IX-143 pp., 1931.
71. ORTH, REV. CLEMENT RAYMOND, O.M.C., J.C.D., The Approbation of Religious Institutes, 171 pp., 1931.
72. PERNICONE, REV. JOSEPH M., A.B., J.C.D., The Ecclesiastical Prohibition of Books, XII-267 pp., 1932.
73. CLINTON, REV. CONNELL, A.B., J.C.D., The Paschal Precept, IX-108 pp., 1932.
74. DONNELLY, REV. FRANCIS B., A.M., S.T.L., J.C.D., The Diocesan Synod, VIII-125 pp., 1932.
75. TORRENTE, REV. CAMILO, C.M.F., J.C.D., Las Processiones Sagradas, V-145 pp., 1932.
76. MURPHY, REV. EDWIN J., C.PP.S., J.C.D., Suspension Ex Informata Conscientia, XI-122 pp., 1932.
77. MACKENZIE, REV. ERIC F., A.M., S.T.L., J.C.D., The Delict of Heresy in its Commission, Penalization, Absolution, VII-124 pp., 1932.
78. LYONS, REV. AVITUS E., S.T.B., J.C.D., The Collegiate Tribunal of First Instance, XI-147 pp., 1932.
79. CONNOLLY, REV. THOMAS A., J.C.D., Appeals, XI-195 pp., 1932.
80. SANGMEISTER, REV. JOSEPH V., A.B., J.C.D., Force and Fear as Precluding Matrimonial Consent, V-211 pp., 1932.
81. JAEGER, REV. LEO A., A.B., J.C.D., The Administration of Vacant and Quasi-Vacant Episcopal Sees in the United States, IX-229 pp., 1932.
82. RIMLINGER, REV. HERBERT T., J.C.D., Error Invalidating Matrimonial Consent, VII-79 pp., 1932.
83. BARRETT, REV. JOHN D. M., S.S., J.C.D., A Comparative Study of the Third Plenary Council of Baltimore and the Code, IX-221 pp., 1932.
84. CARBERRY, REV. JOHN J., PH.D., S.T.D., J.C.D., The Juridical Form of Marriage, X-177 pp., 1934.
85. DOLAN, REV. JOHN L., A.B., J.C.D., The Defensor Vinculi, XII-157 pp., 1934.
86. HANNAN, REV. JEROME D., A.M., S.T.D., LL.B., J.C.D., The Canon Law of Wills, IX-517 pp., 1934.

87. Lemieux, Rev. Delise A., A.M., J.C.D., The Sentence in Ecclesiastical Procedure, IX-131 pp., 1934.
88. O'Rourke, Rev. James J., A.B., J.C.D., Parish Registers, VII-109 pp., 1934.
89. Timlin, Rev. Bartholomew, O.F.M., A.M., J.C.D., Conditional Matrimonial Consent, X-381 pp., 1934.
90. Wahl, Rev. Francis X., A.B., J.C.D., The Matrimonial Impediments of Consanguinity and Affinity, VI-125 pp., 1934.
91. White, Rev. Robert J., A.B., LL.B., S.T.B., J.C.D., Canonical Ante-Nuptial Promises and the Civil Law, VI-152 pp., 1934.
92. Herrera, Rev. Antonio Parra, O.C.D., J.C.D., Legislacion Ecclesiastica sobra el Ayuno y la Abstinencia, XI-191 pp., 1935.
93. Kennedy, Rev. Edwin J., J.C.D., The Special Matrimonial Process in Cases of Evident Nullity, X-165 pp., 1935.
94. Manning, Rev. John J., A.B., J.C.D., Presumption of Law in Matrimonial Procedure, XI-111 pp., 1935.
95. Moeder, Rev. John M., J.C.D., The Proper Bishop for Ordination and Dimissorial Letters, VII-135 pp., 1935.
96. O'Mara, Rev. William A., A.B., J.C.D., Canonical Causes for Matrimonial Dispensations, IX-155 pp., 1935.
97. Reilly, Rev. Peter, J.C.D., Residence of Pastors, IX-81 pp., 1935.
98. Smith, Rev. Mariner T., O.P., S.T.Lr., J.C.D., The Penal Law for Religious, VII-169 pp., 1935.
99. Whalen, Rev. Donald W., A.M., J.C.D., The Value of Testimonial Evidence in Matrimonial Procedure, XIII-297 pp., 1935.
100. Cleary, Rev. Joseph F., J.C.D., Canonical Limitations on the Alienation of Church Property, VIII-141 pp., 1936.
101. Glynn, Rev. John C., J.C.D., The Promoter of Justice, XX-337 pp., 1936.
102. Brennan, Rev. James H., S.S., M.A., S.T.B., J.C.D., The Simple Convalidation of Marriage, VI-135 pp., 1937.
103. Brunini, Rev. Joseph Bernard, J.C.D., The Clerical Obligations of Canons 139 and 142, X-121 pp., 1937.
104. Connor, Rev. Maurice, A.B., J.C.D., The Administrative Removal of Pastors, VIII-159 pp., 1937.
105. Guilfoyle, Rev. Merlin Joseph, J.C.D., Custom, XI-144 pp., 1937.
106. Hughes, Rev. James Austin, A.B., A.M., J.C.D., Witnesses in Criminal Trials of Clerics, IX-140 pp., 1937.
107. Jansen, Rev. Raymond J., A.B., S.T.L., J.C.D., Canonical Provisions for Catechetical Instruction, VII-153 pp., 1937.
108. Kealy, Rev. John James, A.B., J.C.D., The Introductory Libellus in Church Court Procedure, XI-121 pp., 1937.
109. McManus, Rev. James Edward, C.SS.R., J.C.D., The Administration of Temporal Goods in Religious Institutes, XVI-196 pp., 1937.

110. MORIARTY, REV. EUGENE JAMES, J.C.D., Oaths in Ecclesiastical Courts, X-115 pp., 1937.

111. RAINER, REV. ELIGIUS GEORGE, C.SS.R., J.C.D., Suspension of Clerics, XVII-249 pp., 1937.

112. REILLY, REV. THOMAS F., C.SS.R., J.C.D., Visitation of Religious, VI-195 pp., 1938.

113. MORIARTY, REV. FRANCIS E., C.SS.R., J.C.D., The Extraordinary Absolution from Censures, XV-334 pp., 1938.

114. CONNOLLY, REV. NICHOLAS P., J.C.D., The Canonical Erection of Parishes, X-132 pp., 1938.

115. DONOVAN, REV. JAMES JOSEPH, J.C.D., The Pastor's Obligation in Prenuptial Investigation, XII-322 pp., 1938.

116. HARRIGAN, REV. ROBERT J., M.A., S.T.B., J.C.D., The Radical Sanation of Invalid Marriages, VIII-208 pp., 1938.

117. BOFFA, REV. CONRAD HUMBERT, J.C.D., Canonical Provisions for Catholic Schools, VII-211 pp., 1939.

118. PARSONS, REV. ANSCAR JOHN, O.M.Cap., J.C.D., Canonical Elections, XII-236 pp., 1939.

119. REILLY, REV. EDWARD MICHAEL, A.B., J.C.D., The General Norms of Dispensation, XII-156 pp., 1939.

120. RYAN, REV. GERALD ALOYSIUS, A.B., J.C.D., Principles of Episcopal Jurisdiction, XII-172 pp., 1939.

121. BURTON, REV. FRANCIS JAMES, C.S.C., A.B., J.C.D., A Commentary on Canon 1125, X-222 pp., 1940.

122. MIASKIEWICZ, REV. FRANCIS SIGISMUND, J.C.D., Supplied Jurisdiction According to Canon 209, XII-340 pp., 1940.

123. RICE, REV. PATRICK WILLIAM, A.B., J.C.D., Proof of Death in Prenuptial Investigation, VIII-156 pp., 1940.

124. ANGLIN, REV. THOMAS FRANCIS, M.S., J.C.D., The Eucharistic Fast, VIII-183 pp., 1941.

125. COLEMAN, REV. JOHN JEROME, J.C.D., The Minister of Confirmation, VI-153 pp., 1941.

126. DOWNS, REV. JOSEPH EMMANUEL, A.B., J.C.D., The Concept of Clerical Immunity, XI-163 pp., 1941.

127. ESSWEIN, REV. ANTHONY ALBERT, J.C.D., Extrajudicial Penal Powers of Ecclesiastical Superiors, X-144 pp., 1941.

128. FARRELL, REV. BENJAMIN FRANCIS, M.A., S.T.L., J.C.D., The Rights and Duties of the Local Ordinary Regarding Congregations of Women Religious of Pontifical Approval, V-195 pp., 1941.

129. FEENEY, REV. THOMAS JOHN, A.B., S.T.L., J.C.D., Restitutio in Integrum, VI-169 pp., 1941.

130. FINDLAY, REV. STEPHEN WILLIAM, O.S.B., A.B., J.C.D., Canonical Norms Governing the Deposition and Degradation of Clerics, XVII-279 pp., 1941.

131. Goodwine, Rev. John, A.B., S.T.L., J.C.D., The Right of the Church to Acquire Property, VIII-119 pp., 1941.
132. Heston, Rev. Edward Louis, C.S.C., Ph.D., S.T.D., J.C.D., The Alienation of Church Property in the United States, XII-222 pp., 1941.
133. Hogan, Rev. James John, A.B., S.T.L., J.C.D., Judicial Advocates and Procurators, XIII-200 pp., 1941.
134. Kealy, Rev. Thomas M., A.B., Litt.B., J.C.D., Dowry of Women Religious, IX-152 pp., 1941.
135. Keene, Rev. Michael James, O.S.B., J.C.D., Religious Ordinaries and Canon 198, V-164 pp., 1942.
136. Kerin, Rev. Charles A., S.S., M.A., S.T.B., J.C.D., The Privation of Christian Burial, XVI-279 pp., 1941.
137. Louis, Rev. William Francis, M.A., J.C.D., Diocesan Archives, X-101 pp., 1941.
138. McDevitt, Rev. Gilbert Joseph, A.B., J.C.D., Legitimacy and Legitimation, X-247 pp., 1941.
139. McDonough, Rev. Thomas Joseph, A.B., J.C.D., Apostolic Administrators, X-217 pp., 1941.
140. Meier, Rev. Carl Anthony, A.B., J.C.D., Penal Administration Procedure Against Negligent Pastors, XI-240 pp., 1941.
141. Schmidt, Rev. John Rogg, A.B., J.C.D., The Principles of Authentic Interpretation in Canon 17 of the Code of Canon Law, XII-331 pp., 1941.
142. Slafkosky, Rev. Andrew Leonard, A.B., J.C.D., The Canonical Episcopal Visitation of the Diocese, X-197 pp., 1941.
143. Swoboda, Rev. Innocent Robert, O.F.M., J.C.D., Ignorance in Relation to the Imputability of Delicts, IX-271 pp., 1941.
144. Dubé, Rev. Arthur Joseph, A.B., J.C.D., The General Principles for the Reckoning of Time in Canon Law, VIII-299 pp., 1941.
145. McBride, Rev. James T., A.B., J.C.D., Incardination and Excardination of Seculars, XX-585 pp., 1941.
146. Król, Rev. John T., J.C.D., The Defendant in Ecclesiastical Trials, XII-207 pp., 1942.
147. Comyns, Rev. Joseph J., C.SS.R., A.B., J.C.D., Papal and Episcopal Administration of Church Property, XIV-155 pp., 1942.
148. Barry, Rev. Garrett Francis, O.M.I., J.C.D., Violation of the Cloister, XII-260 pp,, 1942.
149. Bolduc, Rev. Gatien, C.S.V., A.B., S.T.L., J.C.D., Les Études dans les Religions Cléricales, VIII-155 pp., 1942.
150. Boyle, Rev. David John, M.A., J.C.D., The Juridic Effects of Moral Certitude on Pre-Nuptial Guarantees, XII-188 pp., 1942.
151. Canavan, Rev. Walter Joseph, M.A., Litt.D., J.C.D., The Profession of Faith, XII-143 pp., 1942.
152. Desrochers, Rev. Bruno, A.B., Ph.L., S.T.B., J.C.D., Le Premier Concile Plénier de Québec et le Code de Droit Canonique, XIV-186 pp., 1942.

153. Dillon, Rev. Robert Edward, A.B., J.C.D., Common Law Marriage, X-148 pp., 1942.
154. Dodwell, Rev. Edward John, Ph.D., S.T.B., J.C.L., The Time and Place for the Celebration of Marriage.
155. Donnellan, Rev. Thomas Andrew, A.B., J.C.D., The Obligation of the Missa pro Populo, VII-131 pp., 1942.
156. Eltz, Rev. Louis Anthony, A.B., J.C.L., Cooperation in Crime.
157. Gass, Rev. Sylvester Francis, M.A., J.C.D., Ecclesiastical Pensions, XI-206 pp., 1942.
158. Guiniven, Rev. John Joseph, C.SS.R., J.C.D., The Precept of Hearing Mass, XIV-188 pp., 1942.
159. Gulczynski, Rev. John Theophilus, J.C.L., The Desecration and Violation of Churches.
160. Hammill, Rev. John Leo, M.A., J.C.D., The Obligations of the Traveler According to Canon 14, VIII-204 pp., 1942.
161. Haydt, Rev. John Joseph, A.B., J.C.D., Reserved Benefices, XI-148 pp., 1942.
162. Huser, Rev. Roger John, O.F.M., A.B., J.C.L., The Crime of Abortion in Canon Law.
163. Kearney, Rev. Francis Patrick, A.B., S.T.L., J.C.L., The Principles of Canon 1127.
164. Linahen, Rev. Leo James, S.T.L., J.C.D., De Absolutione Complicis In Peccato Turpi, 114 pp., 1942.
165. McCloskey, Rev. Joseph Aloysius, A.B., J.C.D., The Subject of Ecclesiastical Law According to Canon 12, XVII-246 pp., 1942.
166. O'Neill, Rev. Francis Joseph, C.SS.R., J.C.D., The Dismissal of Religious in Temporary Vows, XIII-220 pp., 1942.
167. Prince, Rev. John Edward, A.B., S.T.B., J.C.D., The Diocesan Chancellor, X-136 pp., 1942.
168. Riesner, Rev. Albert Joseph, C.SS.R., J.C.D., Apostates and Fugitives from Religious Institutes, IX-168 pp., 1942.
169. Stenger, Rev. Joseph Bernard, J.C.D., The Mortgaging of Church Property, 186 pp., 1942.
170. Waldron, Rev. Joseph Francis, A.B., J.C.D., The Minister of Baptism, XII-197 pp., 1942.
171. Willett, Rev. Robert Albert, J.C.D., The Probative Value of Documents in Ecclesiastical Trials, X-124 pp., 1942.
172. Woeber, Rev. Edward Martin, M.A., J.C.D., The Interpellations, XII-161 pp., 1942.
173. Benko, Rev. Matthew Aloysius, O.S.B., M.A., J.C.L., The Abbot *Nullius*.
174. Christ, Rev. Joseph James, M.A., S.T.L., J.C.L., Dispensation from Vindicative Penalties.
175. Clancy, Rev. Patrick M. J., O.P., A.B., S.T.Lr., J.C.L., The Local Religious Superior.

176. CLARKE, REV. THOMAS JAMES, J.C.L., Parish Societies.
177. CONNOLLY, REV. JOHN PATRICK, S.T.L., J.C.L., Synodal Examiners and Parish Priest Consultors.
178. DRUMM, REV. WILLIAM MARTIN, A.B., J.C.L., Hospital Chaplains.
179. FLANAGAN, REV. BERNARD JOSEPH, A.B., S.T.L., J.C.L., The Canonical Erection of Religious Houses.
180. KELLEHER, REV. STEPHEN JOSEPH, A.B., S.T.B., J.C.L., Discussions with non-Catholics: Canonical Legislation.
181. LEWIS, REV. GORDIAN, C.P., J.C.L., Chapters in Religious Institutes.
182. MARX, REV. ADOLPH, J.C.L., The Declaration of Nullity of Marriages Contracted Outside the Church.
183. MATULENAS, REV. RAYMOND ANTHONY, O.S.B., A.B., J.C.L., Communication, a Source of Privileges.
184. O'LEARY, REV. CHARLES GERARD, C.SS.R., Religious Dismissed After Perpetual Profession.
185. POWER, REV. CORNELIUS MICHAEL, J.C.L., The Blessing of Cemeteries.
186. SHUHLER, REV. RALPH VINCENT, O.S.A., J.C.L., Privileges of Religious to Absolve and Dispense.
187. ZIOLKOWSKI, REV. THADDEUS STANISLAUS, A.B., J.C.L., The Consecration and Blessing of Churches.

www.ingramcontent.com/pod-product-compliance
Lightning Source LLC
LaVergne TN
LVHW050219080826
844660LV00012B/435

* 9 7 8 0 8 1 3 2 2 3 6 5 0 *